LONDON'S
ENGINE SHEDS

Volume 2. The East and South

ROGER GRIFFITHS & JOHN HOOPER

Copyright Book Law Publications – First published in the United Kingdom in 2017

ISBN 978-1-909625-69-3

Printed and bound by The Amadeus Press, Cleckheaton, West Yorkshire
Published by Book Law Publications, 382 Carlton Hill, Nottingham, NG4 1JA

Introduction

The history of London's steam sheds dates from 1836, through to the end of main line steam working in the Capital in July 1967, although London Transport's small fleet of steam locomotives worked on for a further four years. In the course of those 135 years, around 130 steam locomotive sheds and principal locomotive stabling points served the railways of Greater London, but by the period of British Railways in the 1950s – inevitably the era most favoured by latter-day enthusiasts – that number was much reduced. Thus, in putting together a photographic reminder of Greater London's steam sheds, only the days of British Railways will be covered and with the few remaining stabling points being ignored, your authors are left with just eighteen' main' sheds to feature – too many, however, to adequately do justice in a single volume.

Fourteen terminal stations served the Capital and if you ask a non-enthusiast how many were situated south of the River Thames, some might be surprised when they hear just two: London Bridge and Waterloo. Therefore the majority of engine sheds was also to be found north of the Thames, which gave the authors a problem of subdivision – we simply could not just compile two volumes: North London and South London, with the river being the dividing line. Accordingly, working first on the north bank, in a clockwise direction, Volume One covered the area west and north of the city, with this volume featuring sheds to the east and south of the Capital. There, in pre- and post-Grouping terms, were locomotive sheds of the: GER (1); NLR (1); LTSR (1); SECR (1); LCDR (1); LSWR (1); SR (2) – total 8 depots.

If you ever visited any of London's engine sheds then this album will hopefully bring back memories from long ago when steam ruled (nearly) along with dirt, grime, ash and clinker.

Like Volume One, this tome also required the help from a number of people and organisations so we would like to express our thanks to all of them including the Armstrong Railway Photographic Trust, David Dunn, Norman Preedy, and Peter Hands for supplying material from his revised *What Happened to Steam* series. Also to Chris Dunne for the use of copious material gathered from his father's notebooks used during shed visits in the 1950s and 1960s. Thank you gentlemen!

Roger Griffiths, North Cyprus
John Hooper, Manche, France

Front Cover :   BB No.34085 501 SQUADRON and MN No.35028 CLAN LINE grace the yard at Stewarts Lane shed 16th August 1959. *Transport Treasury.*

Rear Cover Top :   A nice rods-down pose as Class H16 No.30519 is seen in quite smart condition at Nine Elms' coaling area on Tuesday 21st May 1957; No.30850 LORD NELSON is a bystander. The tank locomotive was on loan from Feltham to assist with empty passenger stock movements between Waterloo and the carriage sidings at Clapham Junction. This was a not uncommon use for the Pacific tanks when there was less work for them at Feltham, but quite how long such 'loans' lasted is not known. *C.J.B. Sanderson (ARPT).*

Rear Cover Bottom : See page 28.

Frontispiece: See page 78.

STRATFORD

In terms of locomotives allocated to its roster, Stratford was by far and away the biggest engine shed in the British Isles, possibly even, Europe, but many of its engines were out-stationed, some on a long-term basis, at no less than thirteen sub-depots. These served the thickly populated and industrialised area to the north-east of London, which for many years, generated extraordinarily dense commuter traffic.

Stratford depot started off modestly enough, when in 1840, the Northern & Eastern Railway (N&ER), erected a roundhouse (polygon) at Stratford. Four years later the N&ER was leased to the Eastern Counties Railway (ECR), shortly after which a four road straight shed was added to the side of the polygon, with two of the roads passing though into the N&ER building.

The ECR was incorporated into the Great Eastern Railway (GER) in 1862 and nine years later the GER opened a 12-road through shed on a new site at Stratford. A brick building under a northlight roof, with a massive overhead coaling plant, it was given the name 'New' shed, with the polygon continuing it's albeit cramped, existence. In 1887 a separate, six road through shed with twin roof gables, opened on a site adjacent to the twelve road building; it became 'New,' while the twelve road shed was renamed 'Jubilee.' This extension allowed the polygon to be taken out of service, to be incorporated into an expanding Stratford locomotive works.

'New' was extended in length in 1895, and 'Jubilee' was reroofed by the LNER in 1930, at which time the last extension was made at Stratford. This was a two road, gable roof building, dead-end, in corrugated iron and dedicated solely to the housing of the numerous works shunting engines in use – later called Departmental locomotives.

Coded STR by the LNER and 30A by BR, the depot's twelve road building was again re-roofed in the late 1940s and that ended development. East Anglia's lack of indigenous coal supplies ensured that its railways would be early candidates for dieselisation and electrification, so Stratford saw an early closure to steam, that being affected in September 1962. Part of the Jubilee shed had already been replaced by a purpose-built diesel depot commissioned before the end of steam working at Stratford. Today the vast site formerly occupied by Stratford's engine sheds and two works buildings, is covered by leisure amenities, commercial buildings and structures put up for the 2012 London Olympics. A bit like the United Kingdom in a field – one big leisure park!

Stratford shed, or at least part of the 'Jubilee' shed – southern end – towards the end of steam working. The BR Standard Cl.4 tanks had arrived from Plaistow and other former London Tilbury & Southend sheds during the summer of 1962 as 30A was winding down its steam allocation and ramping up the size of its diesel fleet. Nos.80074 and 80075 from the LTS lot are gracing the yard but not for much longer as they would both move on to March depot when steam operations officially ceased in September; both of the 2-6-4Ts went to March but ended their working days in Scotland and then gravitated to one of the Scottish scrapyards. L1 No.67703 remained at Stratford and was condemned on 16th September 1962 along with any other Eastern Region engines of LNER origin including L1s Nos.67716, 67723, 67724, 67729, 67731, 67734, and 67735 (Stratford works did however scrap at least one other L1 brought in from Norwich shed that month!). Seemingly acting with indecent haste to clear the depot of any withdrawn steam locomotives, the L1 and her sisters were hauled away to Doncaster and cut up during November and December. Just out of frame on the left, is the south end of the new four-road diesel maintenance shed which opened a couple of years beforehand and had been built on half the site of this one time twelve road building. What of that coaling plant dominating the right side of the illustration? It was naturally stripped of the coal still in its bunkers (gravity and open wagons doing the necessary) prior to all the machinery and metal parts of the structure being dismantled. By the summer of 1963 the concrete edifice was ready for demolition. Steam at Stratford was finished but we are not so the following pages will be a reminder of what happened at this, the largest motive power depot in Britain, during the days before BR committed to diesel and electric traction. *A. Ives (ARPT)*.

Resident B1 No.61006 BLACKBUCK on the shed yard 26th October 1958 with a long term resident, J39 No.64775, on the left. *I.S. Carr (ARPT)*.

B12 No.61535 and B1 No.61005 BONGO stand on the former 'Jubilee' shed roads (the six-road section of the northern part of the shed had just been demolished to make way for a new four-road diesel depot) in the north yard. The date is early September 1958 and a great transition is taking place on BR and especially here at Stratford where the High Meads locomotive repair shops are undergoing conversion for diesel maintenance and overhauls whilst half of the 'Jubilee' steam shed was removed to build a new double-ended diesel maintenance and servicing depot to look after the needs of the main-line diesel locomotives allocated to 30A. Meanwhile, during 1958 a new depot (No.1 shed) was opened to serve the diesel locomotives already at Stratford until the new shed (2 and 3 sheds) was completed on the site of the 'Jubilee' shed when it became a diesel multiple unit servicing depot. The roof of that 1958 building is visible behind the diesel on the right. That newly delivered North British Type 1 Bo-Bo diesel-electric D8404 is getting attention from the Stratford fitters – the class of ten locomotives would be getting a lot of that over the next ten years before they were condemned! What of the 4-6-0s? The B12 was an Ipswich engine at the time of this photograph and a transfer to Norwich on 1st November 1959 would be its last as it was condemned six weeks later. Evidence of its last 'General' is still visible in its external appearance. Stratford's BONGO on the other hand still had a General overhaul to attend in 1960 and five more engine sheds to serve before its November 1962 withdrawal. *P.J. Robinson (ARPT)*.

Because of the proximity of the locomotive works to Stratford engine shed, it was normal for the engine shed to take charge of any ex-works engines to run them in traffic and prepare them for returning to their home sheds. Such was the case here alongside High Meads shops on Sunday 30th May 1948 where Thompson B1 No.61040 (smokebox numberplate), and 1040 elsewhere about the engine, is being rectified and adjusted (boiler test?) during the latter stages of a General overhaul which started on Monday 12th April and was recorded as completed Saturday 12th June 1948. The 4-6-0 was the first B1 to be built by outside contractors, which was the North British Locomotive Co. in this case and was their No.25796. Put into traffic on Tuesday 16th April 1946, it had the name ROEDEER (a small elegant deer found in the forests of northern Scotland) fitted when released. This overhaul was its first General but it had received a Heavy 10-day repair – 3rd to 13th September 1947 – at Stratford when its original boiler (5062) was changed for No.5067 (ex-1047). This time the B1 had boiler (3704) fitted from B2 No.2832 (No.61632). As can be seen, the engine has yet to be painted but beforehand a few parts have got to be refitted (surely that beat-up specimen on the floor isn't the dome cover!). The four-digit bufferbeam number would disappear but the shed name Norwich might be retained until ER shed plates appear later. Note that the tender has already been painted with the full name of BR applied in the absence of the yet to be finalised BR emblem. *K.H. Cockerill (ARPT)*.

Most unusually, B12 No.61538 and E4 No.62790 glisten in the sun during early April 1950 after receiving Casual Light repairs at Stratford. The Cambridge allocated 2-4-0 had entered shops on 15th November 1949 and emerged four and a half months later on 29th March 1950 after what must have been damage repairs which required a total repaint. Likewise, the Grantham based 4-6-0 went into works on 14th January and emerged 22nd March 1950 after the same class of repair which it appears required a repaint to the standard exhibited after a 'General' overhaul. We get a chance here to see the difference between the small and large versions of the BR lion and wheel emblem. *J.W. Armstrong (ARPT)*.

January 1952 and a trio of diverse classes await attention at Stratford. Yarmouth Beach based B12 No.61545, minus tender, is in for a Casual Light repair, a classified repair which usually means damage/collision repairs; Y4 No.68128 is one of the Stratford shunting fleet and is in for an unclassified repair. Built at Stratford and put into traffic in January 1921, the 0-4-0T spent its entire life working around the Stratford complex. Condemned 8th October 1956, and then cut up here, the Y4 had undergone nine boiler changes during its life, three of those saw new boilers fitted, and the rest were second-hand! It would be interesting to know the mileage clocked up by the 0-4-0T. Finally, at the back of the queue is J69/1 No.68542 which was here for a General overhaul. Resident at South Lynn shed the 0-6-0T was one of the much-travelled members of the ex-GER six-coupled tank fraternity. In January 1929 it left the GE lines and ventured north to Manchester for a fourteen year stint at LNER sheds in the north-west of England including Bidston, Brunswick, Gorton, Trafford Park, and Walton-on-the-Hill, returning south via New England in July 1943. No.68542 finished its career with a two-year residency at 30A. It was condemned 16th September 1962, aged 70 years, and cut up at Stratford where it had all begun in 1892. So in the mix is a stay-at-home next to a nomad. Diverse indeed! *Ken Cockerill (ARPT).*

Y4 No.68128 rigged for work with an abundance of coal. Now, did anyone out there fire one of these? It is Sunday 15th March 1953 and the 0-4-0T was supposed to have entered shops for a 'General' (its last) on the previous Wednesday but it appears that things were running a bit late. Meanwhile someone has to remove all that coal before the Y4 can go into the erecting shop. Over on the left B17 No.61612 HOUGHTON HALL is queueing up ready for its next General overhaul which was due to start on 24th March, at Doncaster! *Norman Preedy.*

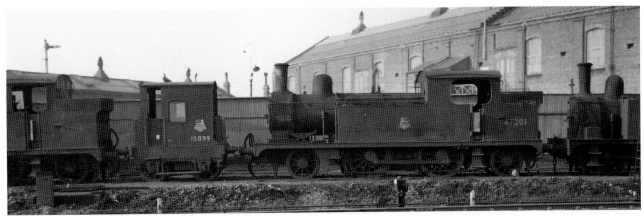

They may be small but F5 No.67201 appears huge compared to Y11 No.15099. F5 No.67219 peeps in from the left whilst an unidentified six-coupled tank stands to the right. The date is 27th January 1957 and all four locomotives are condemned, awaiting scrapping by the Stratford cutting gang. Let's look at the 2-4-2Ts first: No.67201, latterly a resident of Lowestoft, was condemned on 17th December last; No.67219 which started life as an F4 but was rebuilt in 1912 to F6 (a clerical error perpetuated until BR times), and was reclassified F5 by BR on 22nd December 1948. It had been a Stratford engine since 2nd March 1952, shortly before its last General overhaul. It was condemned on 6th November 1956. Both of those engines were Stratford built, did time as residents, and were scrapped there. Y11 No.15099 was much more interesting although it was petrol driven so stay with me. Built in February 1921 by Motor Rail & Tram Car Co. Limited, of Bedford, as their No.2037, it was purchased by the North British Railway on the 23rd of that month (I'm not sure what phase moon was in!) and put to work at Kelso replacing three shunting horses. At that time it had a virtually open cab with a roof but that was in the days when drivers were drivers! Just over seven years later a Sentinel Y1 was purchased by the LNER and that then replaced the Y11 which was sent away to Connah's Quay on 27th June 1928. Just under a year earlier a tall cab structure (as illustrated here) was fitted at Cowlairs during a 'General' overhaul (the days of Scottish drivers enduring any weather were over). It was resident at its North Wales retreat for just six weeks before another job beckoned at Ware which was to be its lot for nearly thirty years. Shortly after arriving in Hertfordshire the four-wheeled motor was damaged by fire and visited Stratford for the first time. Thereafter heavy overhauls and repairs were carried out at either Stratford or the LNER Road Motor Department workshop at Holloway. It was numbered 8431 in the locomotive fleet in July 1930; allocated 7593 under the Thompson scheme of 1943, it never did carry that number but under the 1946 scheme it duly became No.8189 on 23rd June 1946 and then 68189 on the last day of 1948. However, on 7th May 1949 it was renumbered yet again but this time into the BR internal combustion number range becoming 15099 albeit with BRITISH RAILWAYS written on the cab on both sides. The moniker No.15099 was initially painted on each bufferbeam. Whereas at Kelso it had a shed, there was no shelter at Ware and a stub siding was used for parking at weekends. When the 'Lion and wheel' emblem was applied during a near eight-month long 'General' at Holloway in 1953/54 (when a new Crossley engine was fitted), the number was also put onto the cab sides as here. It was condemned on 21st November 1956 and so another class passed into history and oblivion. Besides No.15099, the LNER had managed to acquire a lookalike Y11 from the GER. Its first number was 8430, received in July 1930, and then from 21st July 1946 it was 8188. Following the same course as 15099, it became No.15098 in May 1949 and was condemned on 4th September 1956 after working at Brentwood since September 1925, and Lowestoft P.W. depot beforehand. There was also another Y11 lookalike, No.15097 but it was based in the north-east under the maintenance of Darlington who condemned it in June 1950. *I.S. Carr (ARPT).*

B12 No.61562 looks decidedly tired not to mention rather filthy. The date is 11th August 1951, a Saturday, and the Ipswich based 4-6-0 has just come into works for its penultimate 'General' overhaul. The B12 was built at Stratford, all of its 'shopping' was performed there, and after its condemnation on 8th August 1955, it was cut up at Stratford. However, throughout its life it only worked from Stratford shed for a total of fourteen months; Ipswich, Norwich, and Colchester being its preferred sheds in that order. *Norman Preedy.*

Under repair at the shed on 1st July 1956, resident F5 No.67209 has had its coupling hook removed. The access hatch is still in the open position to give us an idea how the fitters addressed the problems of reaching such fittings, not to mention the front faces of the cylinders. The 2-4-2T was condemned seven months after this tranquil Sunday scene was captured on film. Note the reinforced rubber rings on the floor near the hook; these were the standard LNER method used which allowed the coupling hook (drawgear) to be pulled under load without detriment to the securing nut or coupling links. *C.J.B. Sanderson (ARPT).*

B17 No.61601 HOLKHAM stands outside 'Jubilee' shed on 25th May 1956 ready for its next job. This engine had pursued an on-off relationship with Stratford throughout its life and was allocated to 30A on five different occasions from new. Three of the residencies were of approximately two years duration each but the fourth one was nearly four years. The final allocation lasted just seven months before the B17 was condemned. Collectively, the 4-6-0 spent nearly ten years at Ipswich, the same amount of time at Parkeston, nearly nine years at Stratford, six months at Cambridge, and just four months at Gorton. *Norman Preedy.*

LNER Standard 0-6-0 No.64772 of J39 class is stabled alongside High Meads shops after *nearly* completing a 'General' on Sunday 15th March 1953. The actual completion date was Monday 16th when the 0-6-0 would be handed over to the Running Department for testing and trials; 30A would be happy to get this one up and running because it was one of their own. Amongst the J39 class of 289 engines, only thirty-two were equipped with Westinghouse brakes besides vacuum brakes. Twenty of the Westinghouse engines worked on the GE lines and had been allocated since new, No.64772 was among them. The other dozen J39 so equipped worked in North Eastern Area and had their Westinghouse removed under the Unification of Brakes programme in 1928. However, the story is not so straightforward and one of the GE batch – No.2725 (64778) – had its Westinghouse removed by mistake during overhaul at Darlington in 1935 and was immediately transferred to NE Area. To balance the allocations, one of the two NE Area J39 still fitted with Westinghouse and actually in Darlington shops receiving a 'General' and having the Westinghouse brake removed – No.1457 (64708) – had the overhaul but the brake system was left in situ and the 0-6-0 was transferred to GE Lines at Stratford from 12th November 1935. No.1457 didn't leave shops until 12th December so the date of transfer was probably the date when the *faux pas* was realised and then corrected. So the GE line kept their twenty Westinghouse fitted engines albeit not exactly in numerical order. The front end of No.64772 looks quite busy with Westinghouse standpipe, vacuum standpipe, and heating hose. Now compared with our three GE six-coupled engines just reviewed, this J39 went early being condemned 3rd July 1961; it was cut up at Doncaster. *Norman Preedy.*

Stratford – Sunday 20th April 1952:

34057, 34065, 41984, 47328, 61004, 61005, 61006, 61008, 61056, 61089, 61109, 61119, 61226, 61227, 61232, 61235, 61271, 61285, 61329, 61333, 61334, 61372, 61535, 61546, 61576, 61602, 61607, 61608, 61610, 61612, 61614, 61622, 61628, 61639, 61646, 61650, 61651, 61654, 61660, 61667, 61737, 61745, 61746, 61752, 61754, 61765, 61777, 61778, 61810, 61815, 61817, 61840, 61880, 61946, 61971, 62033, 62036, 62039, 62068, 62506, 62530, 62558, 62791, 64649, 64650, 64651, 64660, 64661, 64663, 64664, 64669, 64670, 64675, 64682, 64686, 64691, 64708, 64764, 64766, 64767, 64769, 64771, 64776, 64777, 64779, 64781, 64783, 64784, 64802, 64803, 64958, 64959, 65422, 65443, 65446, 65449, 65450, 65452, 65454, 65455, 65463, 65476, 65508, 65511, 65518, 65531, 65536, 65538, 65540, 65541, 65543, 65555, 65563, 65564, 65572, 67188, 67194, 67198, 67202, 67204, 67209, 67211, 67212, 67215, 67713, 67721, 67724, 67727, 67730, 67733, 67737, 67792, 68125, 68126, 68128, 68491, 68496, 68508, 68510, 68517, 68519, 68520, 68521, 68526, 68527, 68538, 68546, 68549, 68550, 68556, 68557, 68563, 68569, 68571, 68573, 68576, 68577, 68588, 68590, 68592, 68594, 68596, 68607, 68608, 68612, 68613, 68616, 68617, 68619, 68621, 68626, 68629, 68631, 68632, 68633, 68642, 68644, 68647, 68648, 68650, 68652, 68653, 68654, 68656, 68660, 68662, 68664, 8665, 68666, 68761, 68778, 68950, 68967, 68977, 69483, 69561, 69604, 69615, 69623, 69624, 69630, 69635, 69639, 69652, 69653, 69654, 69655, 69656, 69657, 69660, 69667, 69668, 69672, 69673, 69675, 69693, 69703, 69704, 69705, 69710, 69724, 69730, 69731, 69732, 70000, 70002, 70016, 90087, 90131, 90510. 12103, 12104, 12105   Total: 233.

(*opposite top*) There now follows a selection of images of former Great Eastern 0-6-0 goods engines starting with J17 No.65513 which arrived at Stratford a week before this picture was taken and was condemned straight away. Why is unsure but the date of 26th March 1961 gives us a clue because the engine was due a boiler change and General overhaul. The day of the diesel had arrived on the GE line and the 0-6-0 wasn't going to receive anything but the chop. Still, sixty-one years in traffic with a rebuilding half-way through isn't a bad innings. Now, will any of those pesky diesels achieve that? *Norman Preedy.*

(*opposite centre*) We go back in time now to be introduced to the youngest of our trio. Back to those heady days of Sunday 13th March 1955 when most of the locomotives visiting main works at Stratford would come out of those shops again, sometimes with a fresh coat of paint and a refurbished boiler or perhaps a new one. Meet J19 No.64666 which has just completed a 'General' (31st January to 26th February 1955) and received a new boiler (No.23469) during the event. Allocated to Colchester at this time, the 0-6-0 has now completed its post-shopping running-in period and is ready for working home on Monday morning. It will visit Stratford works again in early 1958 for another 'General' and boiler change. Its final visit to Stratford (it was reallocated to 30A 6th December 1959) was on 13th January 1961 when it was due for another major overhaul but was instead condemned! *Norman Preedy.*

(*opposite bottom*) J15 No.65445 is the oldest (just) of our band of goods engines highlighted here. Amongst the last of her kind, she was built under the Holden regime to a tried and tested Worsdell design, the GER Y14. Not looking its best in this Saturday 25th March 1961 illustration, the J15 appears as though it is joining the other two 0-6-0s on the scrap line but that certainly wasn't the case. It had recently transferred from Parkeston to Stratford (1st January 1961) and was being positioned on the shed yard after the tender had been topped-up for Monday's work load. Withdrawal eventually came on 1st August 1962, a fortnight before the big cull, and No.65445 was scrapped here at Stratford, its place of birth and where, in August 1899 it was first put to work! Note the Type 4 diesel with the dodgy BR crest. *Norman Preedy.*

Ten days after being condemned, F6 No.67229 queues patiently on 28th March 1958 at Stratford for the chop! Latterly of Lowestoft shed, the 2-4-2T hasn't been at Stratford since June 1952 for a change of boiler. The last two members of this once twenty strong class – 67227 and 67230 – were condemned in May 1958. *Norman Preedy.*

No.67716, one of Darlington built Thompson L1 tank engines bathes in the afternoon sun of Saturday 25th March 1961 at Stratford. This engine was put into traffic on 16th April 1948 as No.69015 but on 15th May 1948 it was renumbered 67716 at Stratford. On 14th May 1950 the 2-6-4T was transferred to Ipswich where it settled down for almost nine years. On 11th January 1959 it returned to Stratford, the wave of dieselisation was stronger at Ipswich just then! Shopping was undertaken at both Darlington and Stratford with the former doing the major overhauls and the latter performing unclassified and 'Light' repairs. Condemned on 16th September 1962 with the rest of the Stratford steam fleet, the L1 was taken to Darlington for scrapping in November. *Norman Preedy*.

Displaying one of those outlawed, wrong facing, BR crests, J69 0-6-0T No.68600 defies everything on 26th March 1961 as it goes about its business at Stratford. It was one of those resident engines which remained active at 30A until the end on 16th September 1962. This filthy specimen of a locomotive had started life at Stratford in 1900 but in August 1928 it went on a grand tour of GE sheds before returning to its east London home some thirty years later. *Norman Preedy*.

'Britannia' Pacific No.70001 LORD HURCOMB being readied for a morning run to Norwich, with an express from Liverpool Street, on Sunday 20th April 1952. The much-reported axle-wheel roller-bearings problems suffered in 1951 by certain members of the class whilst working the intensive diagrams devised for the GE line express passenger services, had by this date been virtually resolved although other similar problems were showing themselves during the early months of 1952. All of the engines were back in service by the end of February 1952 but still the doubts remained for some months. One other glitch suffered by certain 'Brits' including those working the GE line, and not often reported, was the failure of the pin securing the engine tender coupling bar (drawgear). No.70012 was parted from its tender and express train at speed in September 1957 after failure of the said pin. A similar incident happened to No.70014 in June 1958 and as a result fixed chains were fitted between engine and tender as recommended in a memo of February 1955 when the problem started showing; how many 'parting' incidents went unreported? On Stratford shed this Sunday were two SR Light Pacifics as noted in the 'engines on shed' list illustrated elsewhere in this section. *Norman Preedy*.

Three months away from withdrawal, a half-respectable looking N7, No.69674 stands in a less than respectable looking yard at 30A on 15th March 1961. Who wouldn't be glad to see the back of all this? Norwich B1 No.61054 stands by the water softener. Even though the 4-6-0 was based at March shed when the time came, it was caught up in the great cull of GE line steam on 16th June 1962 and condemned. The N7 was one of the Gorton-built examples. *Norman Preedy*.

During its gigantic introductory tour of the BR regions, the prototype Deltic went to the London Midland's Western Lines, and the Eastern Region's East Coast Main Line, both events have been extensively recorded before in both words and pictures but little has been published about 'Deltic's' visit to the ER's Great Eastern line. Here we present the big blue Co-Co on Friday 11th March 1960 during a visit to Stratford. Why the prototype came to 30A is not exactly clear. Was it on a demonstration run, or was it a planned visit to High Meads shops (which had recently been modernised to cater for diesel locomotives) as part of the programme of trying out the diesel in various strategic locations prior to accepting the production class on BR? Anyway, what a little beauty! *R.F. Payne (ARPT)*.

Built 1961 to replace an earlier lower capacity crane, this Cowans Sheldon steam crane was one of those retained by BR after steam motive power was eliminated in 1968, and was later (1978) converted to a diesel hydraulic crane with a lifting capacity of 76 tonnes! This is the crane at Stratford on the second day of 1963 near High Meads shops with a sprinkling of seasonal snow (it was the start of a very unpleasant winter) and some nice converted Gresley passenger stock to keep it company. *A. Ives (ARPT)*.

Stratford Shed & Works – Saturday 25th January 1958:
Old works: 43090, 43091, 43092, 61006, 61111, 61399, 61572, 62588, 64647, 64652, 64669, 64708, 64766, 64889, 65520, 65581, 65583, 65589, 69586, 69592, 69647, 69721, 80071,
High Meads: 12110, D3048, 13068, 15213,   Diesel depot: D5503,

M.P.D.
43095, 61109, 61182, 61226, 61233, 61279, 61280, 61300, 61314, 61329, 61335, 61362, 61378, 61384, 61519, 61535, 61556, 61600, 61623, 61629, 61650, 61651, 61652, 61654, 61655, 61658, 61660, 61810, 61831, 61834, 61840, 61880, 61921, 61926, 61951, 61957, 61972, 62032, 62055, 62584, 62619, 62789, 63590, 63773, 63887, 64650, 64666, 64668, 64677, 64680, 64685, 64687, 64694, 64702, 64765, 64767, 64774, 64775, 64779, 64780, 64782, 64783, 64807, 65424, 65433, 65443, 65449, 65450, 65463, 65511, 65522, 65531, 65540, 65572, 65574, 67200, 67203, 67214, 67701, 67724, 67727, 67730, 67733, 67734, 67737, 68510, 68522, 68526, 68532, 68543, 68546, 68549, 68563, 68574, 68575, 68577, 68579, 68591, 68593, 68607, 68613, 68639, 68644, 68652, 68659, 69626, 69643, 69688, 69696, 69729, 69730, 70001, 70002, 70003, 70005, 70007, 70008, 70013, 70030, 70036, 70037, 70038, 70040, 76031, 76033, 76034, 76046, 80077, 90062, 90279, 90298, 90508, 90551, 90660, 11100, D2214, 11121, 11122, 11130, 11131, 11133, 11503, 11508, 12068, 12074, 12109, 12124, 12127, 12135, 13165, 13300, D3499, D3500, D3501, 15211   Total: 183.

Stratford Shed & Works – Sunday 25th February 1962:
61119, 61149, 61156, 61226, 61253, 61329, 61335, 61362, 61375, 61378, 61572, 64657, 64664, 64671, 64673, 65361, 65453, 65457, 65460, 65462, 65464, 65465, 65476, 65521, 65532, 65577, 65583, 67703, 67709, 67720, 67723, 67724, 67729, 67730, 67731, 67734, 67735, 67737, 68499, 68542, 68556, 68565, 68566, 68600, 68609, 68626, 69640, 69653, 69692, 69697, 69725, DS 32, DS 33, DS 44, DS 45, 12106, 12107, 12109, 12130, 12132, D200, D201, D203, D208, D2224, D2226, D2229, D2953, D2957, D3303, D3501, D3632, D3635, D3636, D3681, D3682, D3683, D5054, D5062, D5502, D5504, D5507, D5513, D5516, D5517, D5518, D5531, D5532, D5533, D5537, D5543, D5552, D5558, D5567, D5579, D5587, D5589, D5591, D5592, D5594, D5596, D5598, D5599, D5600, D5616, D5623, D5627, D5633, D5634, D5635, D5669, D5697, D5699, D5800, D5900, D5903, D5904, D6701, D6703, D6713, D6714, D6716, D6717, D6719, D6721, D6724, D6728, D6729, D8024, D8225, D8227, D8228, D8229, D8232, D8233, D8235, D8236, D8240, D8400, D8401, D8402, D8403, D8404, D8405, D8406, D8408, D8409 Total: 147.

Stratford – Sunday 28th April 1963:
61572, 65445, 65462, 65464, 65469, 69621, D202, D205, D206, D208, D2209, D2211, D2216, D2223, D2224, D2225, D2226, D2227, D2553, D2953, D2955, D2999, D3300, D3301, D3303, D3502, D3609, D3632, D3633, D3682, D3683, D4189, D4191, D4192, D5500, D5501, D5505, D5507, D5509, D5514, D5517, D5525, D5544, D5546, D5579, D5588, D5591, D5593, D5596, D5598, D5630, D5658, D5660, D5661, D5663, D5664, D5667, D5693, D5699, D5900, D5902, D5903, D5904, D5906, D5907, D5908, D5909, D6700, D6704, D6708, D6711, D6714, D6716, D6718, D6719, D6720, D6721, D6726, D6728, D8200, D8201, D8202, D8206, D8207, D8208, D8209, D8210, D8212, D8213, D8214, D8215, D8218, D8223, D8237, D8239, D8241, D8242, D8243, D8403, D8404, D8405, D8408, 12104, 12105, 12109   Total: 105.

Tenderless D16/2 No.2553 stabled outside the Old works near Stratford station on Friday 22nd August 1947. The 4-4-0 was one of the 'Super Clauds' introduced in 1923 with a larger boiler. This locomotive started life at Stratford works in November 1906 as what became known in LNER classification as a D15; rebuilt in September 1930 to D16 Part 2 standard with that large boiler, it was again rebuilt in September 1949 to Class D16 Part 3 standard. At the time this scene was recorded, the 4-4-0 had just completed a Light repair and was waiting to be taken across to the shed for coupling up to its tender, lighting up, and being sent home to Ipswich. The GER numbered this engine 1842; renumbered 8842 in June 1924, it was one of the few LNER engines to acquire a Thompson number (7712) in 1942. In March 1946 it was renumbered again to 2553 and then 62553 in May 1948. Throughout its lifetime No.2553 had used seventeen boilers (not unusual in the GER hard water area), of which only two were new; it's first, and last! It worked in the former GE area for the whole of its life, being allocated to just four sheds – Ipswich, Norwich, and Yarmouth, although most of them three or four times at each except the last, Cambridge where it resided for just fourteen months before being condemned on 1st January 1957 and later cut up at Stratford. They liked to keep everything nice and compact at Stratford. The J17 is No.5501 from Cambridge also completing a Light repair after ten days in shops. *C.W. Allen (ARPT).*

DEVONS ROAD, BOW

The small North London Railway (NLR), commenced operations in 1850, gradually extending its services over new lines and also via connections with other railways. Always an all-tank engine railway, the NLR at first bought-in locomotives, but from 1863 constructed its own at Bow Works. Adjoining the works was the NLR's first engine shed, of five roads, but increasing traffic eventually led to a requirement for new accommodation. Accordingly in 1882, on a former brickfield, about a half mile south and backing onto a canal – the Limehouse Cut – the NLR opened a large new engine facility comprised of two, ten-road dead-end buildings in brick, under northlight roofs. The move of engine facilities enabled the first shed to be incorporated into an expanded locomotive works.

The NLR was by then a *protégé* of the LNWR so the new sheds were to the pattern of Webb and were supplemented by a turntable and coaling stage. The sheds were numbered 1 and 2 from west to east, with 1 designated for engines in steam, while 2 was used for those requiring washout, etc. The NLR was worked by the LNWR from 1909 and absorbed by it at the end of 1922 just before all came into the LMS. That company provided a mechanical coaling plant in 1935, just before which No.2 shed had deteriorated such that its roof was missing, leading to the building being dispensed with altogether. The LMS did not codify Devons Road for some time, but in the great reshuffle of the motive power department in 1935, it was designated 13B under Plaistow, which situation continued until 1949 when it became 1D, that code lasting until the end. No.1 shed had been reduced to six roads, with a Louvre type roof in the 1940s.

In 1957 came the BR announcement that Devons Road would be converted into the country's first, all-diesel locomotive shed. That was accomplished on 25th August 1958 when the last operating steam engines were transferred away (some remained in store for a time), and the new fleet of English Electric, British Thompson & Houston and North British, Type 1 Bo-Bo diesel-electric locomotives, along with some shunting types, took over the depot's workings. As it transpired, falling traffic levels and changing patterns saw a rapid decline in the need for Devons Road shed so after less than six years as a diesel depot it closed on 10th February 1964, to lay derelict for a time before it was demolished. The site today accommodates offices and warehousing.

Another one for works! Ex-LT&SR 0-6-2T No.41981 from Plaistow awaits works attention on 22nd September 1957. Former Devons Road 3F 0-6-0T No.47312, another 33A steed now, has accompanied the larger 3F to Bow. Note the lack of a coupling at the front whereas a heating hose is present, in summer, on a designated freight locomotive. Visible in the left background is the mechanical coaling plant provided in 1935. During LMS days Devons Road shed code was 13B, a garage shed of 13A Plaistow. It was altered to 1D after 1948 and remained 1D until closure. Let's not forget the diesel depot adapted here from the steam shed; when the majority of the steam locomotives had been transferred away in October 1957, the contractors moved in and constructed simple wooden working platforms inside the shed and created a screen to partition the working areas. The first diesels arrived in 1957, shunters and then Type 1s from various manufacturers, before work on the shed conversion had even started. However, the work was done and a very steep learning curve was now facing BR and its personnel. *Norman Preedy.*

Devons Road – What was on shed Sunday 11th January 1953:
43001, 43020, 43021, 43022, 43024, 44348, 44441, 44563, 47215, 47302, 47304, 47307, 47314, 47315, 47349, 47350, 47482, 47483, 47486, 47490, 47492, 47493, 47494, 47495, 47497, 47501, 47511, 47514, 47515, 47517, 47558, 47559, 47560, 47561, 47564, 58851, 58853, 58854, 58855, 58857, 58858, 58859, 58861
Total: 43.

Devons Road – What was on shed Sunday 25th February 1962:
D2900, D2901, D2903, D2905, D2907, D8007, D8008, D8009, D8011, D8012, D8014, D8015, D8016, D8017, D8018, D8019, D8041, D8042
Total: 18.

Devons Road – What was on shed Sunday 28th April 1963:
D2900, D2901, D2902, D2903, D2904, D2906, D2907, D8007, D8008, D8010, D8011, D8016, D8017, D8019, D8040, D8041, D8042, D8043, D8044
Total: 19.

Shortly before Devons Road shed was altered and refurbished for the coming of the diesels, 'Jinty' No.47564 has a good head of steam on the afternoon of Sunday 22nd September 1957. Just two months hence the 3F 0-6-0T would make the trek north to Barrow-in-Furness to begin work in a still largely steam environment in what was then known as North Lancashire in the days before the area found itself in Cumbria. In the background, 4F No.44372 was another of the ex-LMS Standards basking in the late summer sun. The 4F was a visitor from Willesden (actually on loan to 1D) but previously had spent a couple of years at Devons Road from April 1951 to June 1953. *Norman Preedy*.

On that same Sunday afternoon in September 1957, the area to the east of the shed, on the stabling roads which were once covered by another ten-road shed, was this get-together of residents. Such a gathering at weekends was usual, as the original ten roads still provided a lot of siding space. Note the elevated water tank which lay at right angles to the erstwhile engine shed and formed a barrier between the depot and Limehouse Cut. The 'missing' shed, which also dated from 1882, was demolished in 1935 as part of the improvements carried out by the LMS when mechanical coal and ash plants were installed at the north end of the shed yard. Ivatt Cl.4 No.43001 was not long for this shed and would transfer to Nuneaton in November 1957 along with the five classmates which came with it in 1951: 43000, 43020, 43021, 43022, and 43024 (*see* later). No.43001 came to Devons Road from Bletchley via Cambridge. *Norman Preedy*.

On Saturday 5th January 1957, class leader of the Stanier ex-LMS 3-cylinder Class 4MT tanks built for the LT&SR section, No.42500, has called into the coaling plant at Devons Road to top up its bunker after a visit to Bow works. The Shoeburyness based 2-6-4T would normally attend the works at Derby for major overhauls but the former North London Railway works at Bow, located just north of the engine shed, was quite capable of carrying out intermediate and heavy overhauls too so when the opportunity arose, the Tilbury line Class 4MTs attended Bow. As early as 1853 a locomotive works was established at Bow by the NLR and some ten years later they had built their first locomotive, a 4-4-0T. Their last building enterprise was in 1906 and that too was a 4-4-0T. Although modern by the standards of the time, Bow was the smallest locomotive works of the LMS Group but its location was useful for maintaining the engines of the NLR and LT&S, not to mention those LMS engines working from Devons Road engine shed. And so until closure in 1960 it remained a useful annex for Derby with all manner of tank locomotives maintained along with 3F, 4F and even Stanier 8Fs passing through the shops. Seems a shame really but that nice recently applied coat of paint was about to receive its first layer of filth! *RAY - 005*.

The so-called LMS 2F 0-6-0T Dock Tanks introduced in 1928 could rightly boast to be amongst the most cosmopolitan of ex-LMS steam locomotives. There were only ten of them built – 47160–47169 (11270–11279 and 7100–7109) – but they were scattered far and wide by the LMS and BR made an even better job. In early LMS days they could be found at Ardrossan, Birkenhead, Dalry Road (Edinburgh), Fleetwood, Greenock, Preston – all dock areas note. By the end of WW2 they had remained at those same sheds except the pair at Ardrossan had moved to Greenock; it was the same by Nationalisation but BR had their own ideas (not least of which was finding suitable employment for the tanks) and started to move certain ones about the system to new and exotic locations. Bidston was one of the fist places but Devons Road and its connections with the Poplar and east London docks were also chosen to host a pair of the 0-6-0T. Nos.47160 and 47164 arrived at 1D separately; 47164 in July 1956 from Bidston, and 47160 in November 1957 from Wrexham via Bidston. In June 1958 with dieselisation pending at Devons Road, the pair departed back to the north and in particular Birkenhead. This is No.47164 at 1D on 5th January 1957 before it was joined by its older sister; note the lack of a shed plate. No.47164 went to other sheds during its remaining years, Sutton Oak, and Speke Junction to name but two. *RAY - 006*.

(above) Another Ivatt 4 at Devons Road but this dirty specimen is wearing the first BR livery as it was delivered to Nuneaton from Horwich in January 1949. The date of this image is 19th July 1952, a Saturday, and the 2-6-0 has been on the 1D roster for just eighteen months and will stay in east London until October 1957. Horwich built the first fifty of this class starting in 1947; they also built another twenty-five during 1951 and '52. Both Darlington (37) and Doncaster (50) turned out more of them between 1950 and 1952. It is interesting to note the various costs charged by the different workshops for separate batches as such: Horwich – Nos.43040–43049: Engine £7,595, Boiler £2,068, Tender £2,184, Total £11,847 each; Doncaster – Nos.43050–43069: Engine £7,629, Boiler £2,777, Tender £2,159, Total £12,565 each; Darlington – Nos.43070–43106: Engine £7,921, Boiler £2,657, Tender £2,195, Total £12,773 each. Now then, what are the preservation people being charged for their various bits? Admitted theirs are one-offs and nearly seventy years separate the costings but inflation has certainly made its mark. Note the double chimney fitted to all fifty of the Horwich-built first batch. They were all later replaced by single chimneys. *RAY - 003. (below)* Sister No.43020 shows off the double chimney on that same July Saturday in 1952. Resident 'Jinty' No.47349 sneaks into view behind. *Norman Preedy.*

An ex-works former LMS to a LT&SR design 4-4-2T, No.41978 on the shed yard at 1D on 19th September 1953. This Plaistow allocated engine had been to Bow works for a spot of work around the smokebox by the looks of things and having been coaled-up is now ready for fire-lighting prior to running the few miles back home. This tank was one of the thirty-five LMS built examples supplied to the London, Tilbury, and Southend line. Initially number 2160, this engine was renumbered by BR so that further examples of the Fairburn 2-6-4T could be built and grouped together numerically. *Norman Preedy*.

Here is one for the diesel fans! D2907 outside the converted shed on an unknown date, so from the following you can perhaps create a date to fit: D2907 arrived at Devons Road from North British Locomotive Co. in August 1958. The last of eight 330 h.p. 0-4-0 diesel-hydraulic shunters earmarked for the depot, it had been preceded by classmates D2900 to D2906 which had started to arrive from Glasgow in late April. This shunter left 1D on 30th November 1963 on transfer to Northampton, afterwards going to Rugby on 2nd October 1965.

Crewe beckoned next and on Bonfire Night 1966 the 0-4-0DH was taken to 5A. The pattern emerging here seems to be a quest for works but just three months afterwards it was all over and on 11th February 1967 it was withdrawn and later that year sold to a scrapyard in Rotherham. Altogether the class consisted of fourteen locomotives; the Devons Road lot minus our subject left for Stratford on 10th February 1964 they then became like a nomadic tribe and moved to various locations in search of that one thing that might save them – work. Crewe locomotive works, and the carriage works at Wolverton were favourite venues but nobody wanted them and they were all withdrawn on 11th February 1967 and sold to a scrapyard in Rotherham in October 1967. What of classmates D2908 to D2913? They all went to work from LM Region sheds from new and continued doing so until – 11th February 1967! Yes, they too were withdrawn and a class of diesel locomotive ceased to exist in one fell swoop. The Slag Reduction Co. at Ickles, Rotherham took a shine to them and so they all ended up in the furnaces of the steel mills of south Yorkshire. *Gordon Turner/GD/ARPT*.

PLAISTOW

Opening its first section in 1854, the London, Tilbury & Southend Railway (LTSR) had complex initial working arrangements with the London & Blackwall and Eastern Counties Railways, and the contractor Peto, Brassey & Betts, to 1875, when the GER took over. Eventually the LTSR came under the influence of the Midland Railway and began a nominally independent existence from 1880, until absorption by the MR in 1911.

At first, the former contractors' sheds at Southend and Tilbury sufficed for the LTSR, thus it was not until about 1896 before the company opened an engine shed alongside Plaistow station. Solidly constructed in brick, the dead end shed covered six roads under three pitched roofs and stood adjacent to the 1880 Plaistow locomotive works. As ever though, traffic increased at a huge rate as rural Essex along the north bank of the Thames came under development. So in about 1911 an eight-road, brick built shed was opened on ground west of the first depot, on the other side of the Northern Outfall Sewer, at which point the six-road building was incorporated into the locomotive works. At first known as 'West Ham' the new dead-end depot was well equipped with four pitched roofs, a ramped coaler, turntable and repair shop and pretty much unchanged, it came into the LMS. In 1930, that company allocated a first code of 34, but in 1935 that was changed to 13A, which continued into BR times, when the depot was moved to the Eastern Region with shed code 33A.

Plaistow shed was subject to wartime damage, made good by the LMS in a flimsy and at the rear, truncated manner and a small mechanical coal hoist was installed in 1955, after which the shed was allowed to moulder away. Plaistow lost its identity on 2nd November 1959 when it became a sub-shed of Tilbury. Steam locomotives continued to visit for turning and watering, etc., until electric working of the LTSR lines commenced on 18th June 1962, whereupon the depot closed. What remained of the buildings was soon cleared away and today the site is utilised for the sports fields of East London Rugby Football Club.

Plaistow shed yard 28th September 1957 with an assortment of tanks, large and small, ex-LMS and BR Standard, and a couple of WD 2-8-0s to help balance the rather top heavy fleet of tanks 'great and small' as highlighted in the April 1954 list where just half a dozen tender engines are shown. Unlikely shed mates in that list were the two ex-GER J17 0-6-0s which were replaced by the WD 'Austerities' in 1955 when the two 0-6-0s had gone back to their native patch by June of that year. Also replaced, but more gradually, was the handful of ex-Midland 2F 0-6-0s which were either withdrawn or transferred, although one in the list was a visitor from Tilbury. The 2-8-0s came to Plaistow in small batches starting with four of them in early March 1955; 90443, 90526, 90668, 90709, which were replaced by four more in May and June of that year: 90196, 90256, 90442, and 90653. In the dying months of 1959 another four WD 2-8-0s joined the second batch for the period whilst the shed was being run-down: Nos.90093, 90106, 90244, 90514; they were all transferred away during those final few weeks when the shed operations were minimalised and 33A became a sub-shed. However, one of them, No.90106 remained behind until 14th November 1959. Reports state that the 2-8-0 was used for clearing out the withdrawn and condemned locomotives ready for the demolition gang to descend on the site but it was some years before the site was cleared as Plaistow operated as a sub of Tilbury until complete closure in 1962. *N.W. Skinner (ARPT).*

Plaistow – What was on shed Sunday 20th April 1952:
41928, 41930, 41939, 41942, 41945, 41948, 41949, 41975, 41980, 41982, 41985, 41987, 41988, 41989, 41990, 41993, 42218, 42219, 42221, 42226, 42248, 42374, 42507, 42513, 42516, 42517, 42522, 42532, 42533, 42534, 42536, 42681, 47262, 47282, 47306, 47311, 47312, 47351, 47429, 47458, 47484, 47512, 47517, 47555, 58054, 58062, 58089, 58191, 58200, 58259, 58310, 65545, 65552, 65566, 65588   Total: 55.

Three 3P 4-4-2T – Nos.41939, 41953, and 41957 – in open, winter, store alongside the main-line at Plaistow shed on Saturday 17th March 1951. The first of them numerically would survive the ordeal and continue to serve BR operations until 1959 when age finally caught up with it. Of the other two, No.41953 was condemned shortly after this scene was recorded whilst sister No.41957 was worked through the summer of '51 but was withdrawn at the cessation of that timetable. The rain soaked yard and overcast is perhaps appropriate for the setting which includes the bridge and embankment carrying the Northern Outfall Sewer as a back drop! *C.J.B. Sanderson (ARPT)*.

We could say that a slow war of attrition was being waged against the ex-LTS Atlantic tanks because No.41930 was another of the class withdrawn in the early 1950s as more of the LMS and BR built Cl.4 tanks were accumulating at the LTS line sheds. This scene was captured on film in March 1952, just one year after Cecil Sanderson's last visit to London; the 4-4-2T was finished by the summer. *C.J.B. Sanderson (ARPT)*.

Before it all went pear-shaped! Plaistow shed yard on 14th April 1957 with a couple of BR Cl.4 tanks – Nos.80100 and 80073 – showing off their handsome lines. Some twenty-eight of the type came new to the LTS line, No.80073 was a Tilbury engine at this time whilst No.80100 was a Plaistow resident. It was one of the LTS based members of the class – Tilbury's No.80103 – which became the first BR Standard Cl.4 to be condemned in September 1962. In the background older pre-Grouping types, No.41992 amongst them, are seemingly still active. Note the rail-enabled conveyor on the ground alongside; it would be interesting to know just how the conveyor worked as regards positioning, and what kind of motive power was used to drive it. From this position in the shed yard we can see the end gable of the shed with that large section of missing roof. It is a wonder the wall stood so long without falling one way or the other in a high wind. *F.W. Hampson (ARPT).*

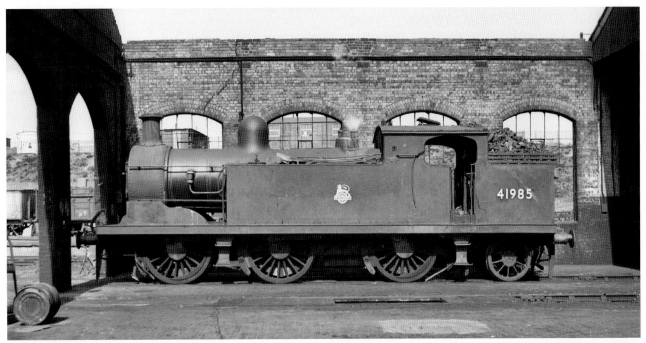

On the same day, 14th April 1957, we have a close-up of the already mentioned roof gap between the end gable and the actual start of the roof. Former LT&S 3F 0-6-2T No.41985 stables in the sun light which is penetrating parts of the building it shouldn't be. All eight of the shed roads still had their arched entrances, albeit in the form of pre-entrances! *F.W. Hampson (ARPT).*

Plaistow – What was on shed Sunday 18th April 1954:

41939, 41946, 41948, 41969, 41980, 41981, 41982, 41983, 41984, 41985, 41987, 41991, 42221, 42224, 42226, 42248, 42254, 42502, 42506, 42513, 42515, 42518, 42529, 42530, 42532, 42534, 42678, 42684, 42687, 47262, 47282, 47300, 47306, 47310, 47311, 47328, 47429, 47458, 47484, 47512, 47555, 58054, 58065, 58089, 58129, 58191, 58200, 58310, 65533, 65566, 80070, 80071, 80074, 80075, 80076, 80077, 80078, 80080.   Total: 58.

Plaistow, Sunday 18th September 1960! The shed, now demoted to sub shed status and for all intents, closed, had become a dumping ground for redundant 2-6-4 tanks. Nearest is ex-LMS Cl.4 No.42508, allocated to Shoeburyness since May 1947 but hidden away, out of service, at its former home (June 1934 to 1941; May to September 1945; August 1946 to May 1947). At other times it had spent most of the war years at Leicester, and at Shoeburyness when not residing at Plaistow; No.42508 remained here until June 1962 when it was condemned then sent to Doncaster some months later where it was cut up in February 1963. In the left background a much younger BR Standard Cl.4, No.80077 is also 'kicking its heels' with nothing to do although the engines here were apparently available for service on their former haunts because full electric services did not start on the LTS line until June 1962. Once that event had taken place the withdrawals started in earnest. However, this particular Cl.4 was engaged in empty stock workings besides permanent way duties during 1961 and '62. When the crunch did arrive, No.80103 made history in late August 1962 when it was condemned at Plaistow with twisted frames and sent to Stratford in September where it was cut-up, the first BR Standard to be so. Its mileage of 281 thousand-odd would suggest it was a third of its way through an operational life. Back to No.80077: in July 1962 it was transferred to Stratford and two months later reallocated to March where it found little or no work for the three months there. Then it continued its northward passage and got to Ardsley in December – sisters 80073–80076 were keeping it company so far but in October 1963 it was time to move on and seeking work, the group ventured forth to Scotland where the first three went to Carstairs. 80076 went to Dumfries, and 80077 ended up at Ardrossan. The others were all withdrawn from their first Scottish Region sheds but 80077 had a final transfer, in July 1964 to Corkerhill. To complete the little saga of that group of Standard 4s, all except 80077 were condemned at the end of July 1964 and were sold for scrap to a firm in Motherwell. No.80077 lasted until 12th October 1964 and she too was sold to that yard in Motherwell. All were less than eleven years old! N.W. Skinner (ARPT).

Further into the bowels of Plaistow shed on that Sunday in September 1960 we find a Whitelegg 3F tank, No.41981 from Tilbury, and another Standard '4', the five years old No.80105, also from Tilbury. Again these two had differing fortunes: the 0-6-2T was withdrawn in June 1962 and hauled away to Doncaster for scrapping whilst No.80105 was taken off to Darlington works and given a General overhaul including a change of boiler in November 1960. It then spasmodically worked the LTS line until transferred away in July 1962 to west Wales where Machynlleth shed beckoned. The duties there were easier than those performed on the Southend line and the Cl.4 was later joined by six of its sisters although No.80105 spent a lot of its time working from Portmadoc sub-shed. Withdrawal of No.80105 took place on 24th July 1965 when the rest of the class still working in the area were made redundant. *N.W. Skinner (ARPT)*.

A half-decent looking No.42511 resides in the semi-derelict shed on Saturday 14th October 1961. BR Std.4 No.80071 is close by and is being inspected by fitters. *I.S. Jones (ARPT)*.

A nicely smoky portrait of Hither Green shed on an unknown date in 1951, with in the foreground, the ash pits leading to the coal stage which is out of sight to the right. Further on from right to left, are the 1938 water softener and water tank adjoining the six-road shed building, with its tracks clearly numbered 1 – 6. Denizens that may be identified are two Q1, two N class, a C 0-6-0 and off to the side, a W class 2-6-4T, a 350hp 0-6-0DE shunter and a visitor from North London, the latter a not uncommon sight at Hither Green. The Johnson MR Cl.3 0-6-0T is condenser fitted, which limits identification to BR numbers 47200 – 47229 and as far as can be discerned, the third and fourth numbers on the cab side are 22. That would totally be appropriate for a locomotive allocated to Cricklewood shed, which routinely worked over London's west circle line, or through the partly underground 'Widened Lines' into Southern territory on inter-regional freights. *K.H. Cockerill (ARPT)*

HITHER GREEN

To serve its new marshalling yard at Hither Green, the Southern Railway opened an attendant locomotive depot on 10th September 1933. The building was dead-ended, of six roads and constructed in concrete with a northlight roof; a double sided ramped coal stage and 65 foot turntable completed the facilities. Like their earlier counterparts at Feltham, the marshalling yard and shed at Hither Green were concerned with freight traffic destined for cross-London destinations and thus was home primarily for goods engines for all its existence.

Because of problems with the water coming to the shed from a well, a water softening plant was installed in 1938 and this marked just about the only change made to the depot. Coded HIT by the SR and 73C by British Railways, the first 0-6-0 diesel shunting locos arrived at the beginning of the 1950s. Indeed, such was the advance of modern traction that it brought about an early closure to steam for 73C, in October 1961. Steam engines continued to visit, however, until total closure to such motive power from 18th June 1962. Following that the shed carried on as a diesel depot until 1990, when it lost its fixed allocation, but still locomotives visited, mostly in conjunction with permanent way works.

The section of shed covering the eastern three roads was taken down in 1993, along with the water tower, but today the shed continues serving as a permanent way depot, with the remaining three road building, a later two road structure and very surprisingly, the turntable still in existence at the extreme north end of the site.

The Class W, three cylinder, 2-6-4T distantly seen in the previous picture is identified in this portrait. Basically a tank engine version of Maunsell's Class N1 2-6-0 but with slightly larger cylinders; the type had parts interchangeable with Classes N, N1, U and U1 and was designed specifically for short-range, inter-company, inter-regional freight traffic around London, a job entirely suited to their great powers of adhesion, starting and haulage – the tractive effort was just shy of 30000 pounds! Fifteen of the class were built, being constructed at Eastleigh and Ashford works and entering service in two batches, between 1932 and 1936. For most of their lives they were shared between just three depots: Hither Green, Norwood Junction and Stewarts Lane, but in BR days, as diesels encroached upon London traffic, the 2-6-4 tanks were sent further afield until all were withdrawn between mid-1963 and Autumn 1964. No.31924 (Ashford, February 1936), was allocated to 73C when this image was recorded, but the engine moved to Feltham, in May 1961, then in November 1962 to Exmouth Junction, leaving there – when the depot became Western Region property in September 1963 – for Norwood Junction. There it stayed for three months before returning to Feltham from where it was withdrawn in July 1964. Of note regarding the engine shed itself, the side of the building has a somewhat temporary air about it and indeed there was enough space on the depot's western edge for another two or three road extension, but such never did come about *K.H. Cockerill (ARPT)*

Hither Green – What was on shed Sunday 18th May 1952:
30688, 30795, 31018, 31054, 31059, 31061, 31063, 31225, 31234, 31245, 31407, 31480, 31687, 31691, 31692, 31695, 31829, 31853, 31856, 31858, 31859, 31862, 31877, 31899, 31900, 31911, 31921, 31922, 31924, 31925, 33031, 33038, 15221, 15222, 15223, 15224, 15225, 15227, 15228, 15229, 15230, 15231, 15232, 15234, 15236, DS1173   Total: 46.

The graceful lines of ex- South Eastern & Chatham Railway (SECR) Class E 4-4-0 No.31159 are seen resting on Hither Green shed on Sunday 22nd October 1950; the engine is bereft of any BR lettering or emblem on its tender side. Designed by Wainwright, twenty-six E class emerged from Ashford works between 1906 and 1909, and were put to work on express passenger duties until superseded in 1914 by the Class L 4-4-0 after which the E's were engaged on lesser passenger workings. Eleven of the type would be rebuilt to become Class E1 and together with the E's, all twenty-six locomotives came into BR ownership. Withdrawals of the Class E commenced in January 1951, with the last being taken out of service in May 1955. This particular engine, No.31159 (Ashford, November 1908), was allocated to Hither Green through its short time with BR, being withdrawn in November 1951; what specific 73C duties it performed are not exactly known. Of additional interest are the diesel shunters stabled by the water tank for the weekend, and an unidentified Class W still bearing the legend SOUTHERN on the tank sides. *K.H. Cockerill (ARPT)*

This portrait of Class N No.31857, gives a good view of Hither Green's coaling stage. This employed a simple, but labour-intensive method for refuelling locomotives, where coal wagons were pushed by a pilot locomotive up the ramp into the top shed. There, fuel was hand-transferred into the half-ton tubs seen in the picture. They ran on narrow gauge tracks, each sitting on a small spur from where they were pushed via a turnplate, at right-angles onto a longitudinal outside track then wheeled to the tippler where another turnplate rotated the tubs, allowing them to be pushed out to the side, for tipping the coal into locomotives' tenders or bunkers. Note that the tub suspended over the tender has the letter G chalked on the side and less discernibly, on the front. Faint traces of chalking may be seen on other tubs, so were those markings a simple alpha series or did some letters perhaps denote tubs with different grades of coal? It is not certain. The date of the picture is unknown, but it is interesting to relate that No.31857 was built in April 1925, assembled at Ashford from a 'kit of parts' produced by, and purchased from, the Woolwich Arsenal. The locomotive carries a 73C shed plate, being allocated to Hither Green between July 1951 and December 1960, so the photograph likely dates from that period; it was withdrawn from Guildford, in April 1964. *C.J.B. Sanderson (ARPT)*

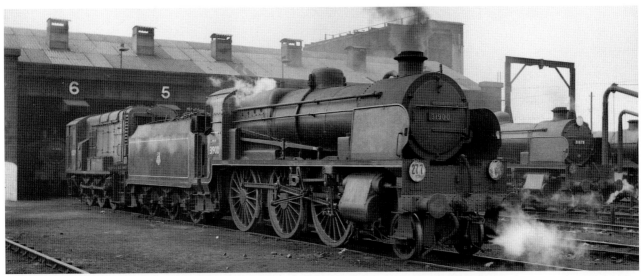

Here is another nice portrait of a Mogul at Hither Green; 3-cylinder Class U1, No.31900 (Eastleigh, May 1931), seen on Sunday 4th May 1957. The 2-6-0 was visiting from Bricklayers Arms shed, from where it would transfer to Stewarts Lane, Salisbury, then to Norwood Junction, where it was withdrawn in December 1962. Other locomotives on view are far right, an unidentified Class W, then N1 No.31879 (Ashford, April 1930), which was a long-term Hither Green resident before moving to Tonbridge in May 1959, then to Stewarts Lane in June 1962, for withdrawal in November of that year. Behind No.31900 is 350hp Bulleid-designed diesel-electric shunter No.15229, from a type that under BR, would have received the TOPS designation Class 12. Ashford-built, the shunter was put to work at Hither Green in July 1951 and remained at the depot until withdrawn in October 1971. The class totalled twenty-six locomotives which should have been built pre-war in 1939 but because of that conflict they did not emerge until April 1949. Cut up at a scrapyard in Newport in 1972, No.15229 was not the last of its class; No.15224 was preserved. Now look at those wheels, where have you seen those before? Lastly, hiding in the shed is Class C No.31691 (Neilson Reid, July 1900), which came to 73C from Faversham in July 1951 and remained until withdrawn in October 1961. *C.J.B. Sanderson (ARPT)*

The shed yard at Hither Green was usually a good place to get panoramic photographs capturing various locomotives. This was so on Sunday 23rd February 1958, when three C class 0-6-0s and three W class W 2-6-4Ts are visible – in whole, or partly. At far left, with the coaling stage headshunt and empty wagons behind, is C No.31510 (Ashford, July 1904), which was visiting from Gillingham shed, later to move via Nine Elms to Bricklayers Arms, from where it would be withdrawn in June 1962. One other C is just visible in the

shed at extreme left, with the third member of that class dominating the picture – No.31573 (Ashford, September 1903). That locomotive had been transferred to Hither Green from Stewarts Lane, in September 1957 and would move on to Feltham, in June 1960, to be withdrawn from there in November 1961. The identifiable members of Class W, Nos.31911 at right and 31912 behind No.31573; the number of the third W, behind 31912, is not known. Nos.31911 and 31912 (Eastleigh, December 1931 and January 1932, respectively), were both allocated to 73C at the time and both would have two simultaneous reallocations: in May 1961 to Eastleigh and from there, in November 1962, to Exmouth Junction. That depot came into the Western Region in September 1963, with code 83D; in the same month No.31911 was withdrawn, while No.31912 returned to the Southern Region at Norwood Junction, where it resided until December 1963 when it made its final move, to Feltham. It was withdrawn in August 1964 along with sister No.31914, thereby rendering the Class W extinct. *Norman Preedy*

Hither Green – What was on shed Sunday 25th February 1962: DS1173,

11221 (D2251), 11228 (D2258), D2180, 15201, 15202, 15216, 15221, 15223, 15226, D3099, D3462, D5000, D5003, D5005, D5008, D5010, D6502, D6508, D6510, D6517, D6519, D6520, D6521, D6523, D6527, D6529, D6530, D6539, D6546, D6548, D6549, D6551, D6555, D6557, D6560, D6568, D6571, D6572, D6573, D6580, D6582, D6585, D6586, D6587, D6588, D6589, D6590   Total: 48.

To judge by the amount of steam coming from locomotives parked around Hither Green shed yard, Saturday 12th March 1960 was a cold day! That did not deter the visiting enthusiasts though, as they processed around the depot collecting numbers, one of which was Class D1 4-4-0 No.31735, a visitor from Bricklayers Arms. In the writer's opinion, there is more than a passing similarity between the D1 and the MR/LMS Class 2P 4-4-0 and this particular engine is interesting in that though designed by Wainwright for the SECR, it was built at the Manchester works of Sharp, Stewart & Company, from where it emerged in November 1901, as SECR Class D No.735. Maunsell had twenty-one of the fifty-one Ds modified with Belpaire fireboxes, the locomotives becoming Class D1 and here again the circumstances were unusual in that some of the rebuilding, including that to No.735, were also carried out in Manchester, this time at the Gorton Works of Beyer, Peacock, during 1921. One Class D1 did not survive WW2, so twenty entered BR service with the last three being withdrawn in November 1961; No.31735 had been taken out of service from Eastleigh shed in April of that year. Of additional interest, seen through the murk, stabled near a Sulzer Type 2 Bo-Bo, was an Eastern Region Class J50 0-6-0T, no doubt from Hornsey shed, that had worked into Southern Region territory with an inter-regional freight. Most likely the J50 would remain for the weekend before heading north over the Thames, on Monday's return to work. *Christopher Campbell.*

Exactly four weeks after the previous picture was recorded, Hither Green is still in the grip of gloomy conditions on Saturday 9th April 1960! But what a cornucopia of C class 0-6-0, were to be seen! Five are on parade outside the shed, plus one partly visible N class. The two 0-6-0 closest to the camera are Nos.31721 and 31268 (Sharp Stewart, January 1901 and Ashford, February 1904, respectively); the first had arrived at 73C in December 1956, on transfer from St Leonards, while No.31268 came to Hither Green, from Nine Elms in January 1960. Both would be transferred to Ashford in May 1961 from where No.31721 was withdrawn in March 1962, with sister 31268 following three months later. The other C facing the camera is No.31717 (Sharp Stewart, January 1901), which was a Bricklayers Arms engine and would be withdrawn from there in February 1962. Lastly, the half-hidden N was No.31874 (Ashford [Woolwich Arsenal], September 1925), also visiting from 73B, which it would leave in December 1961 and move to Exmouth Junction. The N became a Western Region responsibility in March 1963 (when Exmouth Junction was re-coded 83D), and was withdrawn in March 1964. In an earlier caption it was remarked how the spare land on the west side of Hither Green shed might have been earmarked for an extension of the depot. That open space is evident here, behind a Drewry 0-6-0DM shunter, accommodating a pair of stabling roads with what looks to be some form of new building at the rear. *Norman Preedy.*

Spring 1961 and it really is near the end for steam at Hither Green, with the rapid influx of BRCW Type 3 diesels. This view has an air of 'departure' about it with, on the shed roof a smoke vent missing over road No.3, a truncated vent over road No.4 and no sign of movement by steam locomotives. Class C No.31690 (Neilson Reid, July 1900), and N class No.31859 (Ashford [Woolwich Arsenal], April 1925), appear to be in light steam in case they are needed, but it would not be long (May 1961), before the latter moved on, basically surplus to requirements, to Norwood Junction, Brighton and Guildford, before finally going west to Exmouth Junction, where withdrawal came in September 1964. Despite there being very little work for steam at 73C, several Cs were retained for a time for special duties but either such duties did not materialise, or were taken over by the New Order, as in October 1961, No.31690 was transferred to Ashford, where its working life ended in July 1962. *P.J. Robinson.*

A sign, that times, were changing at 73C with three Class W looking quite smart, and fully coaled-up, as they rest at Hither Green during the summer of 1958. However, it seems they may not have been in use as they occupy sidings away from the shed, on the edge of the permanent way depot. At centre is No.31925, the last of the class, built at Ashford in April 1936. The engine was based at 73C for all of its BR years, until May 1961 when it moved to Norwood Junction from where it was withdrawn in November 1963. *K.H. Cockerill (ARPT)*

Sunday 22nd October 1950 and ex-SECR O1 No.1391 looks as if it has been in store for quite a time. Built as a Class O in October 1893 by Sharp, Stewart & Co., it was converted to Class O1 in September 1907. At the time this picture was taken the engine was on Hither Green's books as it were, but it is certain it never worked again as it was withdrawn in June 1951. *K.H. Cockerill (ARPT).*

Having taken a photograph of a sad looking No.1391, Ken Cockerill turned around and took a picture of two more, stored Class O1s. Only No.31258 may be identified but in great contrast to its sister No.1391's early demise, this engine still had a future. Built as a Class O at Ashford in May 1894, SER No.391 would become a Class O1 exactly twenty years later. The locomotive would leave Hither Green in July 1951 on transfer to Dover, from where it would work for almost another decade, before being withdrawn in January 1961, in its 66th year! *K.H. Cockerill (ARPT)*

One of the regular visitors to Hither Green, from 'Norf' London, Eastern Region J50 No.68926 waits its return working on Monday 5th October 1959. The 0-6-0T was allocated to Hornsey, having arrived there from Doncaster shed in October 1958. Once again though, the engine's shed plate has not been changed – doubtless an insignificant task for Hornsey shed when it was in the intense progress of becoming a (mostly) diesel depot. Almost certainly the J50 still carried its Doncaster shed plate when it returned there in July 1961, to be withdrawn in February 1962. Sitting behind No.68926 is Class C No.31698 which had been built by Neilson, Reid & Co. at their Hyde Park Works, Glasgow, in July 1900. The engine had been transferred to Hither Green from Gillingham in June 1951, but by the time this picture was taken may have been out of use as it would be withdrawn in February 1960. *N.W. Skinner (ARPT)*

After capturing an image of No.68926 at Hither Green, Mr Skinner made his way to the east side of the coaling stage where C class No.31298 and W No.31923 were on the disposal road, with a background of the large permanent way depot that lay to the east of the engine shed and still functions as such today, though in a much changed way. No.31298 was a product of Ashford Works in March 1908 and as maybe seen from its freshly painted shed plate, had arrived at 73C that month, from Nine Elms. The change of depot did not long delay the end though as the 0-6-0 was withdrawn in November 1960. No.31923 would move to Feltham in December 1960 and be withdrawn in January 1963. *N.W. Skinner (ARPT)*

All six members of Class N1 were allocated to Hither Green at the start of BR, which makes perfect sense for ease of maintenance, etc., of such a small class. No surprises then when the 3-cylinder 2-6-0s were reallocated *en masse* in May 1959 to Tonbridge, where they saw most use on the route to Redhill and onto the Brighton line. In June 1962 came another mass move, to Stewarts Lane, from where all six locomotives were withdrawn in November of that year. In this spring 1957 illustration, No.31878 (Ashford April 1930) is seen backing off shed at Hither Green. *C.J.B. Sanderson (ARPT)*

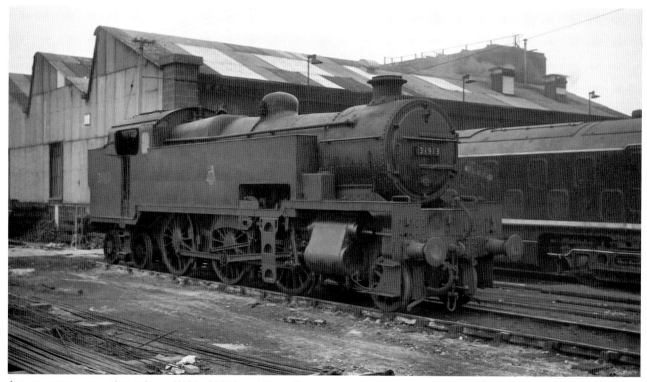

A NOT TO BE MOVED sign adorns W No.31913 at Hither Green, early in 1959. Whether the 2-6-4T was failed in some way, and/or that a fitter was working on it, probably out of sight, is not known, but if it was 'broken' one wonders why much effort would be spent when the locomotive's harbinger of doom – a Sulzer Type 2 Bo-Bo – was ticking away in the background. But repaired it must have been as the W, which was built at Ashford in January 1932, was not withdrawn until March 1964; in that time it would see reallocations to Eastleigh, Exmouth Junction, Norwood Junction and Feltham. *W.R.E. Lewis (ARPT)*

Walking down the shed yard, away from the stopped W (previous caption), Mr Lewis came upon not one, but two J50s visiting from Hornsey depot. Unfortunately he did not log their numbers on his picture so all we have to go on is C class No.31693 and a second un-identified Sulzer diesel. A long-term Hither Green engine, No.31693 was yet another Class C to have been built by Neilson Reid & Co., in July 1900 – see the distinctive oval builder's plate on the centre coupled wheel splasher. The coming of those diesels caused the 0-6-0 to be reallocated to Bricklayers Arms in June 1960, at which depot it ended its days in June 1961. *W.R.E. Lewis (ARPT)*

A change from the usual Hither Green fare of Classes C, N and W, a BR Standard Class 5, 4-6-0 visited 73C on Saturday 12th May 1960. No.73083 had been delivered from Derby Works in July 1955, with its first shed allocation being Stewarts Lane. In May 1959 came a move to Nine Elms where, in October of that year it was named PENDRAGON, with plates from ex-'King Arthur' No.30746. The engine transferred to Feltham in September 1964 and two months later, to Weymouth where it remained until withdrawal in September 1966. The term 'Pendragon' is attributed to early Welsh and means 'Chief Dragon' or 'Dragon's Head'. In one of the earliest writings about Arthurian legend, *Historia Requm Britanniae*, Pendragon is given as the surname of King Uther, who was father to King Arthur. Confusingly perhaps, the Southern Railway also had a 'King Arthur' class locomotive called KING UTHER – No.30737. In the picture's background, being coaled is Class C 31689, a Hither Green engine, that 0-6-0, in October 1961, would transfer to Bricklayers Arms where five months later, it was taken out of service. *Christopher Campbell.*

Hither Green – What was on shed Sunday 28th April 1963: DS 1173,
D2085, D3098, D3466, D3665, D4099, D6510, D6519, D6526, D6529, D6531, D6537, D6541, D6543, D6545, D6547, D6553, D6554, D6555, D6558, D6561, D6562, D6563, D6570, D6576, D6577, D6582, D6584, D6594, 11229, 15201, 15202, 15214, 15215, 15218, 15223, E6003, E6004, E6005
Total: 39

An atmospheric close-up of the lovely Edwardian lines of E3 No.31166; note the early BR livery and buffer beam number, also that the locomotive does not carry what should have been a 73E shed plate on the smokebox door. *Norman Preedy.*

BRICKLAYERS ARMS

This shed had a complex history, starting in the early 1840s when the South Eastern Railway and London & Croydon Railways (SER and LCR), were in dispute with the London & Greenwich Railway (LGR) over the latter's charges for allowing the SER and LCR over its tracks into London Bridge terminus. Accordingly the two aggrieved railways promoted their own spur line to a passenger terminus - albeit inconveniently situated – at Bricklayers Arms. That opened on 1st May 1844 with a two road engine shed provided as part of the complex; the manner of construction of that building has yet to be determined.

In 1852 the dispute with the LGR was ended when all passenger services thereafter ran into London Bridge, leaving Bricklayers Arms to become a goods depot that steadily would be enlarged over the years, to emerge as one of London's largest freight terminals. The engine shed similarly grew with, in 1847, erection of a four road dead-end shed in brick, having a single pitch tiled roof with central ridge vent; it stood some 100 feet north of the two-road building. Next, around 1865 came a second four-road shed adjoining the first along its southern side. The new building was also dead-end, built in brick, with two pitched roofs with central vents, but shorter than the 1847 structure by some 80 feet. A single turntable at the east end, with coaling platforms on each side, gave access to all eight roads.

Matters did not rest long, however, because in 1869, a six-road shed, brick, dead- ended and under two pitched roofs with ridge vents, was installed at the rear of the twin four-road building, but at a right angle to it. The only means of access to what was called the 'New' shed was via a second turntable located at the rear of the twin four-road depot which became known as the 'Old' shed. All four roads of the 1847 structure, and one from the 1865 building, were taken through the rear walls to that turntable; as with 'Old' shed, coaling platforms were provided on each side of the access roads to the 'table. At the same time the original two-road shed, by then out of use, was demolished and four tracks laid over its site into an extension of an existing carriage shed, called 'St. Patrick's.' The origin of the St. Patrick's name has escaped the authors, but it is of relevance because about 1902, that four-road carriage shed section, with a single pitch roof, was adapted for additional locomotive running use.

In a scheme that ran between 1937 and 1939, the 1847 portion of 'Old' and 'St.Patricks,' both were re-roofed by the Southern Railway, with steel framed, asbestos transverse pitches and square smoke vents; at the same time a tub and hoist coaling plant replaced the various coaling stages with the east turntable being removed and the yard thereabouts re-modelled to accommodate the new coaler. Then came WW2, during which the depot was bomb-damaged several times, 'New' especially so, when it lost most of its roof and part of the side walls. That damage never was repaired so through the BR period, after what remained of the roof was taken down, 'New' was a four, then a three road part-walled, open store for engines in steam and for surplus locomotives and coal, rejoicing in the nickname 'The Coal Hole!' The 1865 portion of 'Old' was reroofed about 1950, in the BR style of the times: lightweight steel braces supporting asbestos longitudinal pitches over each road. At the same time a large repair shop was put up on the opposite side of the turntable, replacing a 1934 shop destroyed by bombing. At other times a water softening plant was provided and the turntable enlarged to 65 feet, before the inevitable run-down of the depot began.

Known for much of its life simply as 'The Brick,' the depot was coded 2 under the SECR, to be recoded BA by the SR and 73B by British Railways. Electrification of the Kent Coast lines, and dieselisation, brought an end to 73B's operational life and it closed on 17th June 1962. Parts of the depot, including the turntable and repair shop, persisted along with the large goods depot, but eventually, all that too, was done away with. Today a Royal Mail depot, London Transport bus garage and a number of other commercial premises, sited along Mandela Way, occupy the historic site.

(*opposite top*) Bricklayers Arms 'Old' is seen from the east on Sunday 29th March 1953. The four road section at left is the 1865 building, as re-roofed by BR in 1950; the right hand building was put up in 1847 and is as re-roofed by the SR in 1937/9. The photographer identified five locomotives, seen from left to right: Ivatt Class 2 No.41299 which was almost new, having been delivered from Crewe in November 1951; the 2-6-2T would move to Exmouth Junction in January 1961, eventually to be withdrawn from Eastleigh in October 1966. On road No.3, beside an enthusiast just emerging from the shed, is ex-SECR Class E No.31166, which came out of Ashford Works in July 1907 as SECR No.166. The 4-4-0 had transferred from 73B to Faversham in March 1952 and would be withdrawn from there in May 1955, the last of its class. Then there are three Class C 0-6-0 - those closest to the camera, reading from the shed outwards: 31086 (Ashford, September 1900), a resident of 73B since transfer from Gillingham in April 1951, and where it would remain until withdrawn in October 1961; 31720 (Sharp Stewart, January 1901) which was transferred to Bricklayers Arms from Hither Green in April 1951 and would move to Faversham in January 1954., eventually to end its career at Ashford in October 1961; lastly, No.31090 (Ashford, December 1902), which came to 73B in April 1951 from Gillingham and be withdrawn at the early date of August 1953. *Norman Preedy.*

Bricklayers Arms – What was on shed Sunday 25th February 1962:
31267, 31271, 31305, 31689, 31825, 32341, 34012, 34013, 34014, 34022, 34034, 34068, 34101, 80012, 80034, 80082, 80083, 15213, 15222, D2287, D3468, D5001, D5004, D6512, D6526, D6531, D6541, D6547, D6552   Total: 29.

The west end of 'Old' shed on Sunday 4th October 1959, showing how all four roads of the 1847 section, and one road of the 1865 portion, had been extended through the original dead-end walls, to access the turntable. That is immediately behind the camera and to help orientate, 'New' shed is to the left off the 'table, while the repair shop is behind, on the other side of the turntable; 'St. Patrick's is to the right but not connected to the turntable. The structure at far right of the picture is the water softener standing on concrete legs with a spur going underneath for the sludge wagon; note the stern admonition: NO FIRES TO BE DROPPED HERE! Of note are the five, ex-London Brighton & South Coast Railway (LBSCR) locomotives in residence, two Class E4 and three Class C2X, both types designed by Billinton. One of each may be identified: nearest the camera is E4 No.32472, built Brighton in June 1898 and carried the name FAY GATE before the entire class of 75 engines began to lose their names, after 1906. No.32472 spent its BR years at 73B, until being reallocated to Nine Elms in June 1960; it was withdrawn from 70A in June 1962. C2X No.32528 was built by Vulcan Foundry in October 1900 as one of the LBSCR's Class C2 of fifty-five locomotives. Billinton's successor, Marsh, rebuilt twenty-nine of the C2 to C2X, from 1908, when they became known as the 'Large Vulcans,' and the SR rebuilt fourteen more in the 1920s. No.32528 itself was made a Class C2X in September 1911 and at the time this photograph was taken, had been allocated at Three Bridges since moving there from Brighton in April 1951; the engine would be condemned in February 1961. *Norman Preedy.*

Close-up pictures of 'New' shed in complete condition have so far eluded the writers; not difficult to understand as any such illustration would have to be pre-WW2. The best that may be offered is this view from Saturday 3ʳᵈ May 1952, when the remaining roof portions of the bomb damaged building were still *in situ;* they would be removed within the next few months. Occupying the dilapidated shed was ex-LBSCR Class E4, 0-6-2T No. 32497, which had been built at Brighton in May 1900, first carrying the name DENNINGTON, which was an erroneous spelling, corrected to DONNINGTON in 1905; even then the appellation would be short-lived. The locomotive was at the time based at Nine Elms, having arrived there in August 1951, from Three Bridges and would remain at 70A until withdrawal in November 1959. *F.W. Hampson (ARPT).*

It is July 1954 and Bricklayers Arms' 'New' shed looks a little tidier after removal of the damaged roof. The three roads extant in May 1952 (*see previous illustration*), have been reduced to two, with a narrow gauge, coal-tub track laid over the filled-in number 3 road; the remainder of the shed was in use for storage, mainly of coal. Three locomotives simmer gently, basking in the sunshine; a pair of Billinton's ex-LBSCR E3 0-6-2Ts and an ex-SECR Class H 0-4-4T. The E3s, Nos.32455 and 32453, had been delivered from Brighton in May and April 1895, respectively. The Class E3 was intended primarily for goods

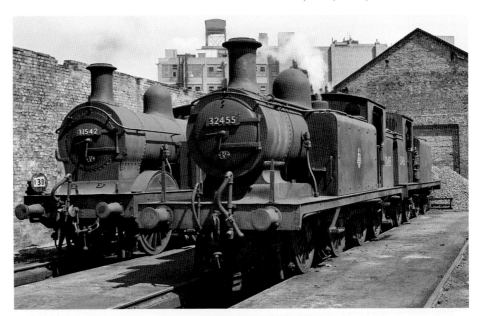

work but when they had undertaken passenger duties such was their good performance that Billinton enlarged upon the design, resulting in the Class E4. As LBSCR Nos.455 and 453 the engines carried the names BROCKHURST and BROADBRIDGE, again until Marsh started to remove names from 1906. At the time this picture was recorded, both 0-6-2Ts were on 73B's roster with No.32455 having arrived from Tonbridge, in January 1951, whilst No.32453 transferred from Eastleigh in July 1953. No.32455 would be the longer-lived, leaving 73B in the next month, for Stewarts Lane, from which shed it was withdrawn in March 1958. Sister No.32453 remained at Bricklayers Arms, being taken out of service in April 1955. The H Class No.31542, built Ashford in November 1904, was a Bricklayers Arms engine, employed mostly on shunting and empty carriage workings; it would reallocate to Dover in November 1956, eventually finding its' was back to London, at Stewarts Lane depot, from where it was withdrawn in November 1962. *K.H. Cockerill (ARPT).*

Bricklayers Arms' turntable – 65 foot in diameter in later years – never was mechanised by vacuum or electric operation. So, although the hand mechanism was geared, the enginemen still had a hard job turning N15 'King Arthur' No.30777 SIR LAMIEL, on Saturday 3rd May 1952, before the engine returned to its home depot at Dover. The large building looming over the turntable at right was the repair shop put up in 1950, while on the left skyline, may be seen a small portion of the northlight roof of 'St. Patrick's' shed, as applied by the SR in 1937/9. No.30777 was one of thirty Class N15 built by the North British Locomotive Company (NBL 23223), at its Hyde Park, Glasgow, works in June 1925; the batch was universally known as the 'Scotch Arthurs' or simply 'Scotchmen.' In July 1936 as No.777, the locomotive hauled a train of ten carriages weighing 345 tons, from Salisbury to Waterloo – 83½ miles – in 72 minutes and 14 seconds, an average speed of 69.2mph. The renowned recorder of locomotive performance, Cecil J. Allen, was aboard the train to witness the event, after which he offered the opinion that this was "probably the most astonishing example of King Arthur ability." With the end of steam in view, BR decided that a member of the King Arthur class should be preserved and it is said that No.777's 1936 flight was the reason the engine was chosen. Leaving Dover in May 1959, No.30777 spent short terms at Feltham and Eastleigh, before being withdrawn in October 1961, with two sisters – both 'Scotch Arthurs' – the last of their class. The N15 joined the National Collection and in later years was restored to working order to run enthusiasts' specials on the main lines. But civil engineering works gradually rendered SIR LAMIEL's former SR routes 'out of gauge' so the engine was relegated to work on preserved railways around Britain. As this is written the engine is based on the Great Central Railway, at Loughborough, in the care of the 5305 Locomotive Association, on behalf of The National Railway Museum. Incidentally, according to Sir Thomas Malory's book on the Arthurian legends, "Le Morte d'Arthur," Sir Lamiel was a knight from Cardiff, renowned as being a great lover! Is it not fitting therefore, that the locomotive was also a good performer? F.W. Hampson (ARPT).

British Railways Southern Region inherited nine ex-LBSCR Atlantics, three of Class H1 and six of Class H2. One H2, (3)2423 THE NEEDLES was taken out of service in May 1949 and the three HI were withdrawn between February and July 1951, but the remaining five H2 were destined to survive somewhat longer. Here, on Saturday 18th March 1950, in early BR livery, Class H2, No.32422 NORTH FORELAND graces the eastern end of Bricklayers Arms shed yard. Coming out of Brighton Works in July 1911 the engine spent all its BR time allocated to Brighton, but out-stationed in the long-term at Brighton's sub-shed at Newhaven. It was withdrawn from there in September 1956 along with sister No.32425; two others, Nos.32421 and 32426 had gone the month before, leaving just 32424 BEACHY HEAD to survive until withdrawal from Brighton in April 1958. The H1 and H2 Class designer was Marsh, who had worked under H.A. Ivatt at Doncaster, so it is little surprise that the LBSCR 4-4-2's bore a strong resemblance to Mr Ivatt's C1 class Atlantics. So much so that when, by a miracle, it was found that a C1 boiler had survived scrapping, it is today the centre of the Bluebell Railway Atlantic Group's efforts to build a replica of No.32424. A rolling chassis has been constructed and work on the boiler continues, so in time it surely will be possible to see an LBSCR Atlantic on the rails again. C.J.B. Sanderson (ARPT).

The fireman has just set the points for Class L1 No.31785 to manoeuvre near Bricklayers Arms coaling plant and is returning to the footplate. It was a dull Thursday 8th July 1954 and to judge by the 'target' indicators on the 4-4-0s front, it seems that the L1 had worked Special train No.87, but it is not known just what that represented – a detail forever lost in history. In 1926, because the Southern Railway's workshops were busy with other work, Maunsell's relatively quick design for additional motive power on the South Eastern section – the Class L1 – were built by the North British Locomotive Company at its Hyde Park, Glasgow workshops. No.31785 had the NBL builder's number 23366. One wonders if the 4-4-0 may have been a bit of a problem child in 1952, as it was reallocated between Bricklayers Arms, Ashford and Eastleigh no fewer than five times, before coming to 73B again, in July 1953. Thus it was on the shed's roster at the time the photograph was taken (see the 73B shed plate), but would move on to Gillingham in May 1955. Upon closure of that depot, in May 1959, No.31785 made its last move to Nine Elms, from where it was withdrawn in January 1960. *F.W. Hampson (ARPT)*

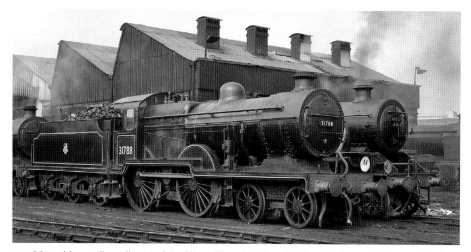

A busy looking Bricklayers Arms on Saturday 2nd October 1954, with L1 No.31788, Fairburn Cl.4 No.42087 and N No.31802 all nicely smoking away; a second 4-4-0 is unidentified. The L1 was built by NBL at Hyde Park Works (builder's number 23369), in April 1926 and had been transferred from Eastleigh, to Bricklayers Arms in June 1954; however, the locomotive retains its 71A shed plate. Whether the plate was eventually changed could have been academic, as from June 1955 the L1 was moved to Dover shed, where it would reside until reallocated to Nine Elms in May 1959; withdrawal followed in January 1960. The LMS design 2-6-4T emerged from Brighton Works in March 1951 and was destined to be moved about a bit! After some time at Brighton and Newhaven depots (the latter was its base at the time of the photograph), No.42087 transferred in June 1956 to Tunbridge Wells West, then to Stewarts Lane, October 1956 to June 1959, returning to 75F. With steam in Kent winding down the locomotive changed allegiances to the LM Region and went to Neasden in December 1959, leaving there when that depot closed in June 1962, for Cricklewood and three months later, Leicester Midland shed. In April 1964, No.42087 was reallocated to Bolton for a couple of months before moving on to Newton Heath. The last move came in July 1966, to Birkenhead, from where the engine was finally withdrawn in October 1966. By contrast, No.31802's future career was much simpler! The 2-6-0 was visiting 73B from Faversham shed, from where it would move in June 1955 to Eastleigh. Its last reallocation would take it to Yeovil Town in June 1960, where in September 1963 it would become a Western Region engine with Yeovil's shed code changing to 83E; withdrawal came in September 1964. *Norman Preedy.*

Another picture from 73B featuring a 4-4-0 and a Fairburn 2-6-4T; the date was mid-1958. Class D1 No.31741 was built by Robert Stephenson & Co., in March 1903, as a Class D; reconstruction to D1 was undertaken at Ashford Works in 1927. The locomotive had been a resident of Bricklayers Arms since moving from Faversham in April 1951, but was in its last year of service, as it was withdrawn in September 1959. If No.42087's odyssey in the previous caption was complex, her sister's was even more so, with no fewer than *twelve* reallocations after leaving the Southern Region. Brighton Works built No.42081 in January 1951, the engine spent three months at Brighton shed before moving to 73B. Then came its trek! December 1959: 14D Neasden; May 1960: 1A Willesden; July 1960: 6H Bangor; September 1960: 9A Longsight; December 1960: 8B Warrington; January 1961: 8A Edge Hill; June 1961: 12C Carlisle Canal; May 1963: 9B Stockport; January 1964: 10B Blackpool; February 1964: 10C Fleetwood; September 1964 10D Lostock Hall; November 1965: 9E Trafford Park; May 1967 withdrawn. *P.J. Robinson (ARPT)*.

A visitor to 73B on Sunday 26th June 1960 was un-rebuilt 'West Country' No.34019 BIDEFORD, then of Brighton shed. Built at Brighton in December 1945 the Pacific was allocated initially to Exmouth Junction depot, but transferred from there to Nine Elms in April 1951, residing until October 1958 and a reallocation to Brighton. From September 1963 would come further transfers to Salisbury, Feltham and Eastleigh, before a final return to Nine Elms, in June 1966 followed by withdrawal in March 1967! The town of Bideford's coat of arms displays three golden clarions above a bridge through which a ship is passing; the motto *PRO REGE AC FIDE AUDAX* translates to: Bold for King and Faith. *Gordon Turner/GD/ARPT.*

A very grubby 'King Arthur' No.30798 SIR HECTIMERE rests at Bricklayers Arms in September 1958, while visiting from Dover. The following month, 74C would become 73H and in May 1959 No.30798 would move to Salisbury. There, the 6-wheel Eastern Section tender would be exchanged for a Western Section bogie tender and in that condition the locomotive would be withdrawn in June 1962. No.30798 was built at Eastleigh in June 1926, but little is known about the Arthurian knight Sir Hectimere – he was but one of many simply mentioned in Malory's *'Le Morte d'Arthur'* in the chapter referring to the illness of Sir Urre of the Mount (30788). *A.R. Thompson (ARPT).*

This picture dates from Saturday 12th March 1960, when 'Schools' No.30927 CLIFTON was one of eight of the class allocated to Bricklayers Arms at the time. The 3-cylinder 4-4-0s worked the dwindling steam-hauled services into Sussex and Kent. Our subject moved to Nine Elms in March 1961 and operated from there until being taken out of service in January 1962. Built at Eastleigh in July 1934, the locomotive was named for the public school situated in the suburb of Clifton in the city of Bristol. Established in 1862 it is one of the original twenty-six English public schools and nowadays is co-educational and known as Clifton College. The school motto is: *Spiritus Intus Alit* (The spirit nourishes within). *Christopher Campbell.*

It is 1947, and the final year of the Southern Railway's existence, as a work-stained N class 2-6-0 No.1404 arrives at Bricklayers Arms shed. The engine came out of Ashford in October 1932 and was based in that town when British Railways came into being. It remained at 74A (later 73F) until January 1961 and a move to Tonbridge, then in May the same year, to Salisbury, where it remained until August 1963 and a final move to Guildford; it was withdrawn in the following December. In the left background and in the right distance, by the elevated water tank, WD locomotives are visible, reminding us that following WW2 they were to be seen working in all sections of the SR into the beginning of the 1950s when those allocated to Southern Region sheds were transferred away. *D.R. Dunn coll. (ARPT).*

On Tuesday 23rd August 1960 it appears as if Bricklayers Arms was hosting a guest from faraway – 6C Birkenhead shed – but not really! Standard Class 4 No.80094 was built at Brighton in October 1954 and went to its first shed at Kentish Town and from there to Bangor in September 1956, before moving to Birkenhead in October 1959. But the stay at 6C was brief as in December that year, 80094 transferred to Three Bridges. So that was where it was based when the picture was taken, but even after eight months it is quite evident that the staff at 75E had not bothered to replace the 2-6-4T's shed plate! *David J. Dippie.*

On the same day as the spurious visitor from Birkenhead, a somewhat grubby C2X No.32552 was simmering in the yard at 73B. Built at Brighton in February 1902 as a Class C2, the locomotive was not modified to C2X until the relatively late date of January 1940. No.32552 had been based at 73B since April 1951 but would move to Norwood Junction in March 1961, from where it would be withdrawn just three months later. *David J. Dippie.*

'Schools' No.30937 EPSOM was not carrying a shed plate when seen at Bricklayers Arms on Sunday 4th October 1959. In fact the locomotive was visiting from Ashford, from where it would move to 73B in May 1961. Five months later the engine would be reallocated to Nine Elms where its career would end in December 1962. Built at Eastleigh in July 1935 the engine was equipped with a Lemaître multiple jet blast pipe, in an experiment by Bulleid. Apparently the modification made little difference to the Schools class' already good performance so only half of the forty 4-4-0s were so fitted. Patronised by HM The Queen, Epsom School is nowadays known as Epsom College. It was founded in 1855 and is renowned because about a third of its alumni entered the medical profession. The school's motto: *Deo Non Fortuna* (Not through luck but by the help of God). *N.W. Skinner (ARPT).*

More shed detail in this picture of Class H 0-4-4T No.31305 laid-up on one of 'New' shed's rubbish-strewn stabling roads, on Monday 14th August 1961. The detail lies in the large repair shop behind the locomotive and the Bulleid tender in front of the H – doubtless the owner of that tender was receiving attention in the workshop. In the distance a part of 'St. Patrick's' 4- road engine shed is seen, but what it important is the lean-to constructed along the north side of that shed for sheltering the depot's breakdown crane; that crane was permanently maintained in-steam, ready to move at a moment's notice of trouble. Then look at the cab of No.31305 and a face, watching the cameraman. If the 'face' was standing, it had to be a very small person – not a juvenile, surely? Or was it perhaps, someone hiding from authority? Whatever! In an environment of 'flat caps', the trilby is an unusual affectation so one may only speculate. The date was 14th August 1961, making No.31305 some 55-years old, (Ashford May 1906), and a resident of 73B since September 1955. In June 1962 the engine would transfer to Stewarts Lane for its final five months' service. *Howard Foster.*

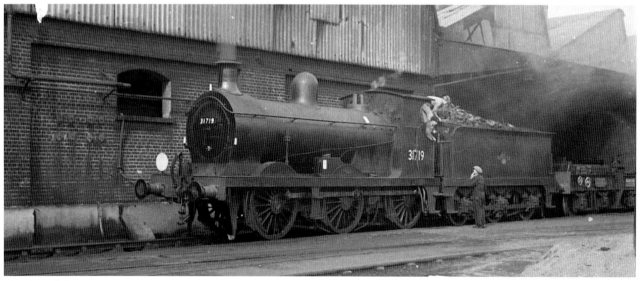

Mention of the breakdown train and the St. Patrick's shed in the previous caption! The cameraman moved down to the shed, no doubt hoping to photograph more locomotives only to find that a problem may have arisen as Class C No.31719 had reversed onto the breakdown train, while the loco crew and a foreman (?) discussed matters; an exercise or the real thing? Unfortunately there was no record to accompany the picture. The Class C had been built in January 1901 by Sharp Stewart and at the time the picture was taken, the 4-4-0 was based at Bricklayers Arms, having arrived there from Stewarts Lane in May 1961; however, the engine still carried a 73A shed plate on the smokebox door. One wonders if that situation changed before the engine was taken out of service in May 1962. *Howard Foster.*

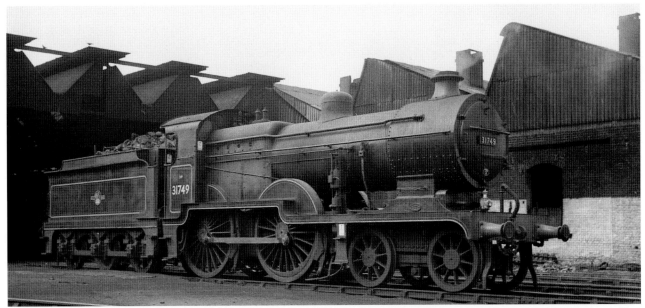

Bricklayers Arms' D1 No.31749 simmers outside the 1865 portion of the Old Shed on Sunday 2nd July 1961. Clearly visible on the side of the smokebox saddle, above the leading bogie, is the Vulcan Foundry 1903, maker's plate when the engine was built as a Class D; it would be modified to Class D1 in 1921, at the Gorton works of Beyer, Peacock & Co. By the time of this photograph there was precious little work for the 4-4-0 to do, so despite looking to be in good order, the engine was withdrawn just five months later. *Howard Foster.*

It may have been noted in other picture captions that there seemed to be a widespread sluggishness about changing smokebox shed plates when an engine transferred between depots! Here is another example with Billinton Radial tank No.32417 at rest in 'The Coal Hole' (New shed) at Bricklayers Arms. The engine had been reallocated to 73B from Norwood Junction, in September 1957, but on Saturday 3rd May 1958, a 75C plate still adorned the smokebox door. Built at Brighton in December 1905, the E6 would return to its birthplace (75A) in May 1961 and be withdrawn in December 1962. Behind No.32417 is Class H No.31540 which had come out of Ashford in November 1904. It had been a Bricklayers Arms locomotive since moving from Dover in April 1951 and would remain at 'The Brick' until leaving service in March 1960. Note that the locomotives are standing on the former No.2 road of New shed; No.3 had been filled-in and was where the sleepers are lying; No.4 is *in situ*, whereas No.5 and 6 have been had their tracks lifted. *W.R.E. Lewis (ARPT).*

The grinning driver knows that he has a true gem in his charge. Britain's last operating Atlantic (tender) locomotive, H2 No.32424 BEACHY HEAD seen at 73B on Monday 12th August 1957. Built at Brighton in September 1911, the engine would remain in service operating from its Brighton base, until April 1958. Its last duty was on the 13th of that month when it hauled the first leg of the R.C.T.S SUSSEX COAST LIMITED rail tour. The Atlantic hauled six coaches and Pullman car Myrtle from Victoria, via Three Bridges and Lewes, to Newhaven Harbour. The remainder of the rail tour was hauled by ex-LBSCR Terrier No.32640 (75A [Newhaven sub shed]), from Newhaven Harbour to Newhaven Town, from where Standard Cl.4 No.80154 – based at Brighton and the last locomotive to be built at Brighton Works (January 1957) – worked from Newhaven Town, via Lewes to Brighton. From there, Ramsgate shed's 'King Arthur' No.30796 SIR DODINAS LE SAVAGE took the special back to Victoria. Challenged to a joust by Sir Dodinas le Savage and Sir Sagramore (30771), together, both were beaten by Sir Tristram (30448). They sought revenge and were again beaten. Later Sir Dodinas would die at the hands of Sir Gareth (30765), his death afterwards avenged by his son Carduin. Christopher Campbell.

A wonderful portrait of an ex-works locomotive as rebuilt 'Battle of Britain' No.34050 ROYAL OBSERVER CORPS rests at Bricklayers Arms in December 1960, having been transferred from Salisbury the previous month. Built at Brighton in December 1946, the Pacific was rebuilt at Eastleigh in August 1958 and would remain at 73B until November 1961 when it was reallocated to Nine Elms. Leaving 70A in September 1964, No.34050 went to Eastleigh from where it was withdrawn in August 1965. The Royal Observer Corps (ROC) was founded in October 1925 composed of a small group of full time professional officers. The ROC served with distinction during WW2, after which it was to be stood down, but the advent of the Cold War ensured that it continued to serve in face of totally new threats. With the end of East – West tensions the ROC was finally disbanded on 31st December 1996. *P.J. Robinson (ARPT)*.

Ramsgate shed's 'Schools' No.30912 DOWNSIDE rests at Bricklayers Arms on Saturday 18th February 1950. The 4-4-0 retains its SR livery, complete with Southern on the tender, but with its BR number on the cab side, in Southern Railway number style; the smokebox number plate is in place but no shed plate. Mention of shed plates, this engine would have seen a number of changes as it transferred between Ramsgate, St. Leonards and Ashford, before finally moving to Nine Elms in June 1959. It remained at 70A until being taken out of service in December 1962, thirty years and three months after coming out of Eastleigh Works. Behind No.30912 is an unidentified sister, seemingly in a darker livery! Downside School, near Shepton Mallet, was founded in 1606 by Benedictine monks who still run the school today along with Lay staff. Catering for children aged between 11 and 18, the school motto is: *Apud bonos iura pietatus* (Among the good, Piety is the law). *C.J.B. Sanderson (ARPT).*

Having photographed No.30912, Cecil Sanderson walked over to the other half of the Old shed and captured this broadside view of C class No.31297; the 0-6-0 was appearing in yet another mix of livery with British Railways on the tender and with its cab side number in Southern-style figures. The 0-6-0 was a 73B locomotive, and would remain until being reallocated in May 1957 to Gillingham, leaving there with the Kent Coast Electrification in May 1959, for Nine Elms; No.31297 was withdrawn in September 1959. Of note, behind the Class C, a Bulleid Pacific in Malachite green livery and just getting into the picture at left, the bunker of H 0-4-4T No.31324. That was another Bricklayers Arms engine which, in November 1951, would transfer to Faversham and be further reallocated six times, before ending its days in July 1962, at Three Bridges shed. *C.J.B. Sanderson (ARPT)*

On Saturday 12th October 1957, Cecil Sanderson paid another visit to 73B and was rewarded by the sight of a resident ex-works E4 0-6-2T No.32474. However, when Mr Sanderson developed the picture he noticed a glaring error – can anyone spot it, before reading further? In 1957 British Railways introduced a new crest for its locomotives, the famous lion within a crown, holding a wheel – but in this picture the crest on the right side of the locomotive is the wrong way round! It is said that BR assumed the lion should face forward on both sides of the engine – but no! In fact, it came to the attention of the College of Arms, the official heraldic authority for England, Wales, Northern Ireland and much of the Commonwealth, including Australia and New Zealand, and that august body was not amused! Very rapidly the word went out across BR to make sure that the new crest was applied correctly on both sides of the locomotives – but there were further transgressions all over BR, the expensive transfers needed to be used up and used they were (*see* the section on Nine Elms shed)! The correct way was: left is right, right is wrong. LBSCR No.474 left the works at Brighton in October 1898 carrying for the first few years, the name BLETCHINGLY and at the beginning of BR was based at Bricklayers Arms, not moving until August 1961 when it was reallocated to Three Bridges. It left there in April 1962 for Brighton where it was withdrawn in May 1963. *C.J.B. Sanderson (ARPT)*

Maunsell's last design was the Class Q 0-6-0, envisaged as a replacement for the many aged 0-6-0s inherited by the Southern. In fact, the first of the class was delivered in January 1938 after Maunsell had retired and although his successor, Bulleid, did not at all like the Class Q design, he allowed the initial order for twenty to be built at Eastleigh in the period up to September 1939; after that Bulleid brought out his own, renowned Class Q1 0-6-0. The Q can generally be considered to have been a success, especially after Bulleid fitted multiple blastpipes to some members of the class and later, BR introduced an awful looking stovepipe chimney and even Standard Cl.4 chimneys – so the twenty locos presented a number of appearances! Here we see multiple blastpipe-fitted, Q No.30538 resting at Bricklayers Arms on Monday 14th August 1961, visiting from its home depot, Brighton. The 0-6-0 would move in June 1962 to Stewarts Lane and from there, six months later, to Bournemouth, from where it was withdrawn in July 1963. *Howard Forster.*

A nice broadside of WC No.34003 PLYMOUTH on Tuesday 23rd August 1960. *David. J. Dippie.*

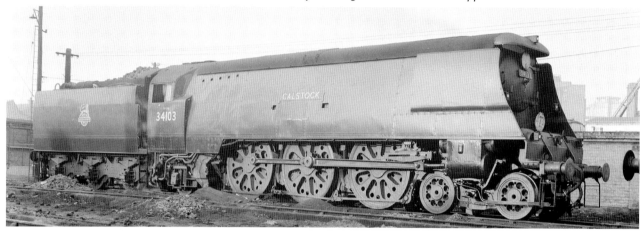

WC No.34103 CALSTOCK on 14th October 1956, new to Stewarts Lane in February 1950, the Pacific transferred to Dover shortly after this image was recorded. *I.S. Jones (ARPT).*

Rebuilt 'West Country' No.34014 BUDLEIGH SALTERTON takes water on Tuesday 23rd August 1960. The engine was built at Brighton in November 1945 and would be modified in March 1958, at which point it was transferred from its long-term residence at Exmouth Junction to Bricklayers Arms. In July 1962 No.34014 would return to 72A, moving from there to Salisbury in September 1964 with a relatively early withdrawal – for a Modified Pacific – in March 1965. The coat of arms displayed above the locomotive's nameplate was a later addition as the crest was not officially granted to the Devonshire town of Budleigh Salterton until 15th December 1959. In typically modern style the coat of arms' motto is *BEAU SEJOUR* – Have a beautiful stay. *David J. Dippie.*

A trio of 'Schools' from various periods show off an assortment of livery and number schemes, along with presentations of cleaning, Bricklayers Arms style. Top to bottom are Nos.30924 HAILEYBURY; 30917 ARDINGLY; 30925 CHELTENHAM on 9th April 1960. *David J. Dippie. Norman Preedy.*

Seen on Saturday 3rd May 1952 is 73B's tub and hoist coaling plant with, behind, the long shed provided to afford cover to the coal wagons, sand store and the men operating the plant. C class No.31293 was in the process of taking on fuel after its last duty. The 0-6-0 had been built at Ashford Works in June 1908 and was a Bricklayers Arms engine for all its BR days that ended with withdrawal in May 1962. *F.W. Hampson (ARPT)*

L1 4-4-0 No.31787 on an unrecorded date. *K.H. Cockerill (ARPT)*.

H class 04-4T No.31324 on 18ᵗʰ February 1950. *C.J.B. Sanderson (ARPT).*

Ivatt Cl.2 No.41299 was one of those wonderful 2-6-2T which came a little late for BR operations. Put to work on all the regions except the Scottish, the tanks were very useful and well-liked engines wherever they went, the comfort of the cab, especially in winter, was one of their many positive features. This example at Bricklayers Arms came direct to the SR from Crewe in November 1951 and remained on the region until withdrawn at Eastleigh in October 1966. *C.J.B. Sanderson (ARPT).*

NINE ELMS

This shed had the most varied history of any London depot, with no fewer than six separate buildings being brought into use over the years. First was a three, possibly four road, dead-ended shed opened by the London & Southampton Railway (LSR) on 21st May 1838. Located on the north side of the main line, south of what would later become the huge Nine Elms (North) Goods Depot, the LSR building became LSWR property the next year, to serve until 1865 and removal. The second shed, opened by the LSWR in 1849, occupied a site to the north east of the first depot; it was of six roads and also served until 1865; it was then removed and the ground covered by part of Nine Elms Goods (North).

Replacement for the first two sheds in 1865 was a building unique in layout for Britain. It stood south of the main line some hundreds of yards west of the first two sites, adjacent to the expanding Nine Elms locomotive works. The uniqueness lay in the shed being of seven through roads, but those tracks were served by no fewer than four turntables and four coaling stages; two of each at both ends of the building. That edifice served for just eleven years though, to be removed and replaced by yet another shed unique in layout. Opened in 1876, on a new site south of Nine Elms works, was a semi-roundhouse of twenty-six roads, served thirteen and thirteen, by two turntables located a few feet from each other with a single connecting spur; a double-sided, ramped coaling stage served one track on each side, accessing each turntable. Such a design of multiple-turntable, open roundhouse was familiar in Europe, especially in Germany, but as far as Britain went, it remains the only example.

The fifth shed for Nine Elms was a massive LSWR 'glasshouse,' a design pioneered at that time and repeated at other locations, in varying sizes. Basically it comprised high pitched roofs of steel braces supporting predominantly glass panels, supplemented with steel and glass gable ends. The building put up at Nine Elms in 1885 lay west of the roundhouse, and was again, unique in its way! It was of fifteen dead-end roads under five pitches, with all roads terminating on a *single* turntable in the extreme southern corner of the depot's site; a large new double sided coaling plant accompanied this building.

The sixth and final shed came about as a result of the move of the LSWR's locomotive works to Eastleigh in 1909. The roundhouse was reportedly closed at the same time, but later Ordnance Survey maps show it still *in situ* and apparently its last traces were not removed until 1923. The roundhouse's replacement was a ten road dead-end shed in brick, with a multiple transverse pitched roof. It came into use in 1910 and adjoined the fifteen road building along that shed's east wall, thus presenting a vista, when seen from the front, of a twenty-five road depot, but names were allocated of 'Old' to the 1885 building and 'New' to the 1910 structure. During WW2 the fifteen road section was damaged sufficiently enough for its roof to permanently be cut back by about a half and for the glass panels to be replaced by asbestos. Even this partial covering would dwindle to almost nothing by the end of steam.

Various improvements were added over the years: a water softening plant was installed, the turntable was increased to 65 feet, and a large mechanical coaling plant appeared in very early BR times. Coded NE by the SR, British Railways allocated code 70A, which was carried through to closure on 9th July 1967 with the end of main line steam running to and from London. By then the buildings were very tired so they soon were removed and today the New Covent Garden Fruit and Vegetable Market occupies the site.

The widest shed in London, at twenty-five roads, of which twenty are seen here. And it must be remembered, ALL of those roads were accessed from a *single* turntable – so it *never* had to break down! At right is the 1910, ten road section and at left, 'three and a bit' of the five, three road sections of the 1885 'Glasshouse,' with two of Battersea power station's four iconic chimneys in the background. Norman Preedy had obviously separated himself from the group of visiting enthusiasts (*see* the party, far right), so he could capture this picture without lots of bodies in view on Wednesday 14th October 1959! Even so, only two locomotives may be identified: ex-LBSCR E4 No.32498 and H16 No.30516. The E4 was built at Brighton in May 1900 and was one of eleven of the type that served with the ROD, in Europe, 1917–1919. When first built it carried the name STRETTINGTON, but as remarked in other captions, Marsh systematically did away with the LBSCR's earlier naming policy – which in this writer's view, was a pity. Anyway No.32498 was a Nine Elms engine all through BR times, mostly engaged upon empty carriage stock (e.c.s.) workings and shunting, not being withdrawn until November 1961. The H16 was on spasmodic loan from Feltham depot, being used primarily for e.c.s. duties too, before it transferred to Eastleigh in January 1960, only to return to Feltham in May 1961 and withdrawal six months later! *Norman Preedy.*

Almost immediately after BR was formed it undertook a widespread series of trials of engines from all the 'Big Four' (the so-called Locomotive Exchanges), to try and assess what were each design's good qualities, with a mind to building a fleet of 'Standard' engines incorporating the best features of all. The Southern Region provided three 'Merchant Navy' Pacifics and three 'Light' Pacifics for the trials, but as much of the testing would be over routes equipped with water pick-up troughs, of which the Southern had none, their engines were temporarily attached to LMS Stanier 4000 gallon tenders, which were fitted with water scoops. One of the chosen Light Pacifics, 'West Country' No.34005 BARNSTAPLE, is at Nine Elms on Saturday 17th July 1948, complete with its Stanier tender in black with white lettering while the locomotive was in SR Green with SR-style numbering. This particular engine was trialled over the former Midland Railway route between London (St. Pancras) and Manchester (Central) with a Nine Elms crew guided by LMR pilot men. The picture was taken on a somewhat wet and windy day, hence the canopy flapping in the top portion of the photograph. But, what was that mysterious box, with handle, sitting on the ground? Perhaps it was a case for a large format camera that Mr Sanderson forgot to move out of frame? 21C105 was built at Brighton in July 1945 and went first to Exmouth Junction shed where is still was based at the time of the Exchanges. Eventually it was rebuilt in June 1957 and operated from Bricklayers Arms, Stewarts Lane and Salisbury depots before finally moving to Brighton in October 1965, from where it was withdrawn in October 1966. *C.J.B. Sanderson (ARPT).*

The early days of BR could provide a sometimes, rich vein of old types of locomotives in their last days of service. One such is seen at Nine Elms on Saturday 10th September 1949: Class N15X No.32333 REMEMBRANCE. The 4-6-0 was built in May 1922 as a Billinton-designed LBSCR Class L 4-6-4T, carrying the name, in honour of the dead of WW1. In service, the Ls were found to be unstable at speed due to water surging about in the side tanks, but despite successful modification to eradicate the problem, all seven of the class were rebuilt to 4-6-0 tender engines of Class N15X at Eastleigh, in 1934. No.32333 retained its name while the others commemorated SR-constituent locomotive engineers. The rebuilt engines were in some ways inferior to the existing 'King Arthurs', so they soon were relegated largely to semi-fast workings and by the beginning of BR all were at Basingstoke depot where their main duties were such passenger trains to London and back. Because they had 'nothing special' going for them and they were a small class in numbers, all seven N15X were withdrawn between 1955 and 1957; No.32333 itself succumbed in April 1956. *C.J.B. Sanderson (ARPT)*

Nine Elms – What was on shed Sunday 15th June 1952:
30123, 30132, 30160, 30244, 30457, 30485, 30521, 30522, 30523, 30692, 30699, 30718, 30719, 30721, 30724, 30750, 30751, 30781, 30853, 30933, 31265, 31320, 31550, 31552, 31619, 31750, 31798, 32498, 32499, 32500, 34007, 34005, 34008, 34011, 34063, 35008, 35010, 35011, 35014, 41293, 15213, 15216, 15218, 15219, 15235   Total: 45.

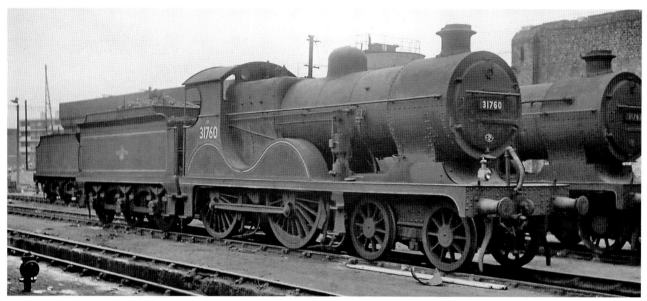

Summer 1960 and the influx of BR Standard steam types had rendered many older locomotives redundant, whereupon they were stored, pending an uncertain future. Two are seen here at Nine Elms: L 4-4-0 No.31760 and beyond, L1 4-4-0 No.31787. The L was built by Beyer, Peacock & Co., in August 1914 and had been based at Tonbridge through its first BR years, coming to 70A in May 1959 and probably immediately stored. It would be withdrawn in June 1961. No.31787 was built by the North British Locomotive Co. in 1926 (maker's number 23368) and spent its BR time working from Bricklayers Arms, Ashford, Eastleigh and Horsham, before its final move to Nine Elms in May 1959. The engine remained in store until withdrawal in January 1961. *W.R.E. Lewis (ARPT).*

There are some varied stories to be told about this very mixed line-up of engines at Nine Elms, on Sunday 4th October 1959. The furthest identifiable locomotive is the stored doyen of Class L1 No.31753 (NBL 23356/1926), which had transferred to 70A from Dover in May 1959; it would not again turn a wheel in revenue-earning service, being withdrawn in October 1961. Next is Standard Cl.5 No.73113 which, two months hence, would receive the name LYONESSE, ex-'King Arthur' No.30743. The Class 5 had been delivered new to Nine Elms, in October 1955, from Doncaster and would remain at 70A until reallocated to Eastleigh in August 1964 and from there to Weymouth in October 1965; withdrawal took place in January 1967. The familiar lines of a GWR 0-6-0PT come next. Eleven of the type had come to the SR in March 1959 and one more in October of that year. Six went to Dover's sub-shed at Folkestone for working the steeply graded harbour branch and six came to Nine Elms to replace older SR types – mainly M7s – on passenger stock workings and shunting. Interestingly all of the Panniers were from the 4600 – 4699 number range except this one, No.9770, which had been built at Swindon in 1936 and arrived at 70A from Laira shed. In July 1963 No.9770 would move west again, to Bath Green Park, from where it would be withdrawn in November that year. Lastly is 'King Arthur' No.30457 SIR BEDIVERE, a product of the Southern's locomotive works at Eastleigh in April 1925. The 4-6-0 had been a bit of a nomad, frequently moving between Exmouth Junction and Salisbury sheds until coming to Nine Elms in June 1951. Then came reallocation to Basingstoke in September 1957, only to return to 70A in May 1958; withdrawal took place in May 1961. In Arthurian legend, Lyonesse was the home of the hero Tristan; it was an island off the coast of Cornwall that later sank beneath the waves. Sir Bedivere was Marshal to King Arthur and it was he who returned the sword Excalibur to the Lady of the Lake, following Arthur's death. *N.W. Skinner (ARPT).*

Here is another Nine Elms line-up on Friday 24th July 1964, a brooding but wonderful portrait of engines and the men that cared for them, going about their many tasks. Rebuilt 'Merchant Navy' No.35025 BROCKLEBANK LINE was BR-built, leaving the works at Eastleigh in November 1948; it would be rebuilt in December 1956. BR allocations were Stewarts Lane, Exmouth Junction and Bournemouth before a last move to 70A in February 1964; withdrawal was at the relatively early date of September in the same year. That was not the end though as the locomotive was saved and is today at a private site at Sellidge, Kent, where it is slowly being brought back to running order. BR Standard Cl.5 No.73111 was delivered new to Nine Elms in October 1955, from Doncaster and in December 1960 would receive the name KING UTHER from 'King Arthur' No.30737. The Class 5 remained at Nine Elms until being transferred to Eastleigh in August 1964 from where it was withdrawn fourteen months later, not even ten years old. Rebuilt 'West Country' No.34010 SIDMOUTH was built at Brighton in September 1945 and after an initial period at Exmouth Junction, was transferred to Nine Elms in April 1951, where it remained until September 1964 when it moved to Eastleigh. During that time – January 1959 – it was rebuilt, and survived until withdrawal in March 1965. The Brocklebank shipping line was formed at Whitehaven in 1801, the offices moving to Liverpool in 1819. Mostly engaged in traffic to the Orient, the line saw many ships lost in WW2, then drastic cuts to its trade with India and Pakistan after 1947. Finally, the 1967–1971 closure of the Suez Canal, and containerisation, led to the company's demise in 1983. In Arthurian legend, King Uther (Pendragon) was Arthur's father – see a related caption for locomotive No.73083 in the section on Hither Green. *A. Ives (ARPT)*

At the beginning of BR, Nine Elms had three, Class O2 0-4-4T which spent their time on general pilot duties; they were: Nos.30179, 30204 and 30212. Very soon that trio departed to be replaced by a single O2 No.30221 which was withdrawn in August 1953, to be replaced by sister No.30224, from Exmouth Junction. That was the last O2 to be based at 70A as when it was withdrawn in February 1958, classes M7 0-4-4T and ex-LBSCR E4 0-6-2T carried out pilot duties until ex-GWR Pannier tanks arrived in 1959, later handing over to BR Cl.3 2-6-2T. A commendably clean No.30224 poses against a background of Nine Elms shed's 1910 building and mechanical coaling plant on Sunday 8th May 1955; it had been built at Nine Elms works in October 1892. *F.W. Hampson (ARPT).*

THE FLEET'S IN! - In this section we concentrate upon the 'Lord Nelson' Class 4-6-0 at Nine Elms. In 1925 R.E.L. Maunsell was tasked with providing an express passenger locomotive capable of hauling 500 ton trains at 55 m.p.h. and after considerable research the prototype No.850 was produced by Eastleigh in August 1926. The decision was taken to name the engines after prominent British admirals, with the first, very obviously being *Lord Nelson*. Classified LN the 4-cylinder type had the unusual feature of its cranks being set at an angle of 135 degrees, which resulted in the engines emitting eight exhaust beats per revolution of the driving wheels – the best description of the resulting sound being that the 'Nelsons' never 'blasted' – they 'puttered'! (There would be a solitary exception in No.865 SIR JOHN HAWKINS, which had cranks set normally and therefore gave out the usual four exhaust beats per revolution).

After two years of trials fifteen more Class LN were constructed between May 1928 and November 1929, but the performance of the class was not as expected, so Maunsell tried out various modifications, like fitting 6ft 3in. wheels to No.859 LORD HOOD, instead of the standard 6ft 7in. and applying a twin Kylchap blast pipe to No.860 LORD HAWKE; smoke deflectors also helped cure a common, drifting smoke problem. When Bulleid took over from Maunsell in 1938 he fitted all the class with Lemaître multiple jet blast pipes, which improved performance considerably and the class settled down to giving good and reliable service operating from three depots: Nine Elms, Eastleigh and Bournemouth.

However, the post-war advent of Bulleid's many Pacifics – and especially their rebuilds – would render the Lord Nelson class largely redundant so all were withdrawn between August 1961 and October 1962. No.30850 was saved for the National Collection and in subsequent years was restored to working condition for hauling enthusiast's special trains over England's network – even as far north as Carlisle. At the time of writing *Lord Nelson* is in the care of the Mid-Hants Railway in non-operational condition.

No.30850 LORD NELSON (September 1758 – October 1805; Battles of The Nile and Trafalgar) photographed Tuesday 21st May 1957. Built August 1926, withdrawn August 1962. *C.J.B. Sanderson (ARPT)*

No.30857 LORD HOWE (March 1726 – August 1799: Jacobite Uprising, American Revolution, French Revolution) photographed Tuesday 21st May 1957. Built December 1928, withdrawn September 1962. *C.J.B. Sanderson (ARPT)*

No.30858 LORD DUNCAN (July 1731 – August 1804; Battles of Cape St. Vincent and Camperdown) photographed Tuesday 21st May 1957. Built January 1929, withdrawn August 1961. *C.J.B. Sanderson (ARPT)*

No.30860 LORD HAWKE (February 1705 – October 1781; War of Austrian Succession, Seven Years' War) photographed Saturday 15th June 1957. Built December 1929, withdrawn August 1962 *C.J.B. Sanderson (ARPT)*

Nine Elms – What was on shed Saturday 15th February 1958:

30245, 30478, 30482, 30486, 30488, 30491, 30512, 30523, 30694, 30699, 30701, 30718, 30763, 30770, 30774, 30778, 30826, 30851, 30852, 30855, 30857, 30860, 30903, 30905, 30906, 31617, 31621, 31634, 32497, 32498, 32500, 32560, 33017, 34008, 34009, 34010, 34011, 34018, 34020, 34033, 34044, 34049, 34055, 34090, 35002, 35003, 35009, 35023, 35025, 73110, 73112, 73113, 73114, 73117, 75074
Total: 55.

Nine Elms – What was on shed Sunday 25th February 1962:

3633, 4616, 4634, 4672, 4681, 4698, 9770, 30035, 30051, 30241, 30249, 30320, 30501, 30831, 30860, 30912, 30935, 30936, 30937, 31612, 31613, 31624, 31636, 31796, 31801, 31803, 32472, 32473, 32487, 32557, 33004, 33014, 33017, 34001, 34007, 34020, 34029, 34044, 34071, 34082, 34093, 34095, 34102, 35005, 35007, 35012, 35013, 35016, 35024, 35028, 35030, 73081, 73082, 73085, 73086, 73112, 73113, 73118, 80084, 15215, D2288, D3096, D3225, D3469
Total: 64.

Urie's first design of locomotive for the LSWR was the H15 4-6-0, intended for fast heavy freight work, but also capable of handling passenger trains. Twenty-six of the type was built in batches over the period 1913–1925, and they served their purpose well with all the class coming into BR use. Generally they were divided between Nine Elms, Eastleigh and Salisbury sheds and not until sufficient quantities of BR Standard types had been brought into service did the H15 begin to bow out; withdrawals starting in April 1955, with the last survivor going at the end of 1961. Here we see No.30488 having its grate cleaned out on Tuesday 21st May 1957; it had been built in March 1914 and was withdrawn in April 1959. The large boiler, correspondingly squat chimney and running plate raised over the cylinders, were distinguishing features of the type. *C.J.B. Sanderson (ARPT)*

With its normal daily throughput of locomotives, Nine Elms' coaling plant was always busy and in the final years surrounded by a huge mess of tipped ash! Here is a typical scene from the summer of 1960, as two rebuilt Light Pacifics have been refuelled and shortly will be despatched to the fire cleaning and ash disposal area. Note the two rows of truncated concrete blocks, they were the former supports for the double-sided coal stage put up with the 1910 ten-road shed extension. 'West Country' No.34046 BRAUNTON and 'Battle of Britain' No.34062 17 SQUADRON, were visiting London from Bournemouth and Exmouth Junction, respectively. The first named had been built at Brighton in November 1946 and then rebuilt in February 1959; it would remain at 71B until withdrawn in October 1965. As is well known the locomotive was saved for preservation and is today owned by Jeremy Hosking; it is currently passed for main line running. No.34062 left the works at Brighton in May 1947 and was rebuilt in April 1959. It too would remain at the one depot, being withdrawn from 72A in August 1964; this engine did not survive the breaker's yard. 17 Squadron RAF took part in the Battle of Britain, flying Hurricanes, from Debden, Tangmere, and Martlesham Heath. In the spring of 1941 the squadron moved to Scotland for a rest before reassignment to the Far East; its crest motto was: *Excellere Contende* (Strive to excel). *Norman Preedy.*

Further away from the coaling plant but still ash aplenty! 'West Country' No.34094 MORTHOE looks splendid in the sunshine of Saturday 15ᵗʰ June 1957. BR-built, coming out of Brighton in October 1949, the Pacific was stationed at Bournemouth until February 1958 when it was transferred to Nine Elms; therefore in this picture it was still a 71B locomotive. That move to 70A was its last as No.34094 was taken out of service in August 1964, to be scrapped. *C.J.B. Sanderson (ARPT).*

Nine Elms' turntable, like its coaling plant, was very heavily worked, seeing that it was the only access to and from the depot's twenty-five shed roads – it is amazing that such an 'all eggs in one basket' state of affairs was maintained! On Saturday 15ᵗʰ June 1957, in original condition, 'Merchant Navy' No.35005 CANADIAN PACIFIC is just about to run off the turntable and make its way off shed to work a train. Built Eastleigh in December 1941, rebuilt December 1960, the Pacific was a Nine Elms engine and would remain so until November 1959 when transferred to Bournemouth, followed by a final reallocation in August 1964 to Weymouth. The engine did not see out the days of steam, being withdrawn in October 1965, but it was preserved and is now owned by the Mid-Hants Railway that for some years ran it on the main line. Currently the engine is in the long process of being restored to running order again. Behind the Pacific are the flats in Brooklands Road, put up in the early 1950s to replace housing destroyed by WW2 bombing. What a wonderful vantage point for watching activity at the shed, but no doubt the housewives had other things to say when hanging out their washing to dry! Brooklands Road was the only official entrance to 70A and it was well policed by the turntable crew in their hut beside the gate; if you did not have a permit it was 99% sure you would not get in! However, there was another way. At the rear of the fifteen-road section of the engine shed was a stonemasonry works which on a Sunday was closed but not locked at all. So by committing outrageous trespass, keen train-spotters could make their way past funeral and other stone edifices to the back of the depot where enough windows at a low level had little glazing. Here the trusty duffle coat acted as a protection against broken glass and hey presto, you got in and then tried to remain invisible – happy days! The Canadian Pacific Steamship Company was founded in 1887 in Vancouver, an offshoot of the Canadian Pacific Railway. At its height the shipping line was Canada's largest operator on the Atlantic and Pacific routes; the former bringing many immigrants from Europe to Canada. Its ships names were usually prefixed *Empress of,* and no fewer than twelve vessels were lost in WW2, including the largest ship to be sunk by a German U-boat, the 42,350 ton *Empress of Britain.* The post-war coming of widespread air travel caused massive change in transatlantic travel so the Canadian Pacific Steamship Company eventually became part of the Hapag-Lloyd conglomerate. *C.J.B. Sanderson (ARPT).*

'ROUND (THE) TABLE' **In this section we concentrate upon the 'King Arthur' Class at Nine Elms.** Urie designed a new passenger 4-6-0 with 6ft 7in. wheels, the first three of which came from the L&SWR's locomotive works at Eastleigh in the latter half of 1918; they were followed by a further seven during the following year. Unfortunately the new locomotives designated Class N15 and named after kings, knights, characters and places of Arthurian tales, were not an initial success with indifferent steaming. When Maunsell succeeded Urie he set about redesigning the N15's front end especially by enlarging steam and exhaust ports, and modifying the blastpipe and chimney; all of which considerably improved performance.

Maunsell had his own designs on the drawing board but to meet short term demand for the traffic in summer 1925, an order for thirty 'Arthurs' was placed with the North British Locomotive Co. of Glasgow. These were very quickly delivered and as remarked earlier became known as the 'Scotch Arthurs' or 'Scotchmen.' At the same time Eastleigh produced ten more of the type though they and other batches – bringing the class total to 74 – had smaller cylinders and higher boiler pressure. In time Bulleid also applied modifications and overall the King Arthur class gave excellent performances for much of their existence. As for their naming, it was an early masterpiece of public relations with the travelling public and in time, with legions of railway enthusiasts!

No.30453 KING ARTHUR, summer 1956. (THE king from whom all else stemmed; nothing more needs saying). Built February 1925, withdrawn July 1961. *R.F. Payne (ARPT).*

No.30452 SIR MELIAGRANCE, Tuesday 20th May 1958. (Sir Meliagrance committed treason by lusting after and imprisoning, Queen Guinevere [30454], but she was rescued by Sir Lancelot [30455] who, with the assistance of Sir Lavaine [30773], killed Sir Meliagrance). Built July 1925, withdrawn August 1959. *C.J.B. Sanderson (ARPT).*

No.30770 SR PRIANIUS, summer 1958. (Sir Prianius was a descendent of Alexander and Hector; whose father had rebelled against Rome. Prianius met the previously un-stoppable Sir Gawain [30764] in combat and stopped him, but only by wounding; he then joined Gawain and fought to defend Arthur, became a Christian and was made a Duke). Built June 1925; withdrawn November 1962 *Gordon Turner/GD/ARPT*.

No.30774 SIR GAHERIS, July 1959. (Sir Gaheris was a nephew of Arthur and younger brother of Gawain and Agravaine [30775]. In the *Lancelot and the Grail* cycle of tales, Gaheris meets his death at the hands of Lancelot, as the latter rescues Queen Guinevere from burning at the stake). Built June 1925, withdrawn January 1960. Also seen is No.30765 SIR GARETH who appropriately, was younger brother to Sir Gaheris and like Gaheris he met his death during Lancelot's rescue of Queen Guinevere, but at the hands of Sir Bors de Ganis [30763]. Built May 1925, withdrawn September 1962. *P.J. Robinson (ARPT)*.

The fireman has cleaned the last remnants of dust from the footplate and shovelled then onto the ground beside rebuilt 'Merchant Nay' No.35015 ROTTERDAM LLOYD. The date is Thursday 18th August 1960 and it looks as if the engine is 'brewing-up' outside Nine Elms' 1910 building, in preparation for leaving the shed and pick up its next train. There were residential areas on three sides of Nine Elms depot and a standing exhortation in force, for locomotive crews not to make (too much) smoke – in this instance perhaps, the success rate could be classed as – low! The Pacific had been built at Eastleigh in March 1945 and would be rebuilt in June 1958. Apart from a three year stint at Stewarts Lane, May 1956 – May 1959, No.35015 was based at 70A for all its BR days, until withdrawn in February 1964, to eventually be scrapped. Formed in 1839 and eventually concentrating on Rotterdam – London – Dutch East Indies traffic, Rotterdam Lloyd underwent many changes until the end of WW2 and the Dutch East Indies' independence, when passenger services were ceased. Eventually the company became part of the large, present day, Hapag-Lloyd conglomerate. *David J. Dippie.*

The remaining west wall of the cut-back 1885 building at Nine Elms forms a backdrop to Class E4 No.32486 one of the depot's general shunting and carriage pilot engines. The date is Tuesday 20th May 1958 eighteen months after the E4 had been transferred to 70A from Salisbury. However, despite looking to be in good condition, the expected arrival of ex-GWR Pannier tanks early in 1959, would render such elderly locomotives as the E4 redundant; No.32486 was withdrawn in January 1959. The 0-6-2T was built at Brighton in May 1899, initially carrying the name GODALMING. *C.J.B. Sanderson (ARPT).*

Officially, Light Pacific No.34090 was a member of the 'Battle of Britain' class though the name did not directly reflect that particular conflict. Instead it honoured Sir Eustace Missenden who became General Manager of the Southern Railway in 1941 and most competently guided it though the tumultuous years of WW2. The nameplate itself is unique, with his name at the top and Southern Railway at bottom with a lower row stating 'Battle of Britain Class'. In the centre is the Missenden family coat of arms with the motto: *Vestigia nulla retrorsum* (No stepping back). SIR EUSTACE MISSENDEN, SOUTHERN RAILWAY was built at Brighton in February 1949 and rebuilt in August 1960. It was sent to the South Eastern Section at first, working from Ramsgate and Stewarts Lane sheds, before coming to Nine Elms in June 1957. A final move to Eastleigh would be made in September 1964, until withdrawal in July 1967; No.34090 went afterwards to the breaker's yard. *N.W. Skinner (ARPT).*

Looking somewhat tatty, BR Standard Cl.5 No.73118 awaits its next job at Nine Elms on Thursday 18th August 1960. It carries the name KING LEODEGRANCE which it received in February 1960, ex-'King Arthur' No.30739 and would bear that name through its remaining service. Built in December 1955 at Doncaster No.73118 came new to Nine Elms, staying until transfer to Eastleigh in August 1964, only to return to 70A in June 1966, before a final move, in September that year, to Guildford. It was withdrawn with the end of Southern Region steam, on 9th July 1967. King Leodegrance was ruler of Cameliard, which usually is supposed to have been in southwest England, but may have been in Britanny, near the present-day town of Carhaix. Leodegrance was an ally of King Uther Pendragon, and father of Guinevere, who was to become queen to King Arthur. *David J. Dippie.*

'SCHOOLS OF THOUGHT' In this section we concentrate upon the 'Schools' Class at Nine Elms. Without question, the 3-cylinder 'Schools' Class 4-4-0 was Maunsell's finest design. Indeed, it was arguably the best 4-4-0 type ever seen in Britain, setting levels of performance and reliability that many types of larger locomotive would have been hard put to beat. The design came about because of a need for a powerful locomotive that could operate on the width restricted lines of the Southern Railway's routes from Chatham to Ramsgate and Tonbridge to Hastings. The 'Schools' featured a high pressure boiler – 220 lbs/sq.in – generated from the largest possible firebox that could be accommodated on the narrow routes. Add to that a front end which proved to be exceptionally free running and you have all the ingredients for the type's success.

In another very clever public relations exercise the locomotives were named after English public (i.e. private!) boarding schools, which given the very class-conscious British system of the time, was inspired. The first engine left Eastleigh in March 1930, followed by several batches, up to August 1935, to total forty locomotives. They gave Sterling service all through their lives and were sent to the breakers' yards only because of the influx of BR Standard steam types, followed by electrification and dieselisation of the routes commonly operated by the class.

Two engines, seemingly from Bricklayers Arms and Stewarts Lane depots are seen on Nine Elms shed in May 1961. In fact, although 4-4-0 No.30931 KING'S WIMBLEDON carries a 73B shed plate, it had been transferred to 70A in March 1961, following a month at Feltham, after no less than fifteen years at Bricklayers Arms. Once again, a shed plate had not been changed after two changes of depot and probably never would be, as the locomotive was withdrawn in September 1961. The 0-6-0T seen beyond the 'Schools' is ex-LBSCR E2 No.32103, which was actually in transit from 73A, to its new home at Southampton Docks shed, to which it had been transferred in the current month. The E2 had been built in December 1913 and would work in Southampton Docks until withdrawal in October 1962. King's Wimbledon School was founded in 1829 as the junior department of Kings College London. It still offers schooling today from its site on Wimbledon Common; a Church of England establishment, its motto is *Sancte Et Sapienter* (With holiness and wisdom). *A.R. Thompson (ARPT).*

Those shed plates were a constant source of confusion! Single-chimney No.30935 SEVENOAKS basks in the sunshine at Nine Elms on Saturday 27th October 1962, wearing a 73B Bricklayers Arms depot plate. However, it had left 73B for Ashford, on 14th June 1959 and then came to Nine Elms on 9th November 1961, so the Bricklayers Arms plate is no less than forty months out of date! Once again it is most unlikely the situation was corrected; No.30935's time was limited as it would be withdrawn in December the same year. Built in June 1935 the engine was a long-term resident of Bricklayers Arms, from new, until moving to St. Leonards in September 1949. Sevenoaks is the second oldest non-denominational school in England, being founded in 1432 as a boys' school but today it is co-educational. The motto is *Servire Deo Regnare Est* (To serve God is to rule). *Howard Foster.*

A lovely, sunlit broadside view of No.30902 WELLINGTON, at Nine Elms, Friday 29th June 1962. The engine had been at 70A since November 1960 and would see out its days at the depot until withdrawal in December 1962. Situated in Wellington, Somerset, the school had opened in 1837, for boys, but like most such establishments eventually became co-educational (1972). The school motto is: *Nisi Dominus Frustra* (the opening of Psalm 127: If God Be Not With Us, Our Labour is in Vain). *Norman Preedy.*

Perhaps having a chat with a Pannier tank, No.30910 MERCHANT TAYLORS, quietly simmers at Nine Elms on Thursday 18th August 1960. The engine had come to 70A in June 1959 from Ramsgate, after no less than twenty-four years of rotating between St. Leonards and Ramsgate depots – mostly spending time at the former, however. As with the other 'Schools' featured here, No.30910 had only a short time left, with withdrawal in November 1961. Merchant Taylors School is another with a long heritage, being founded in 1561 at the Manor of the Rose, but later occupying a number of sites in central London, before moving to its present location at the 285 acre, Sandy Lodge, Northwood in 1933. Still an independent boys' school, the motto is: *Concordia parvae res crescunt* (Small things grow in harmony). *David J. Dippie.*

A nameless 'Merchant Navy' alongside un-rebuilt 'Battle of Britain' No.34057 without a number plate, with a BR Standard Cl.5 in the same predicament. It could only be Nine Elms in 1967 – see over for more melancholy scenes. *P.J. Robinson (ARPT)*.

One benefit of all Britain's railways coming under a central management was that if a major problem occurred for a time, there was a much wider field of resources from which to make interim arrangements. For example, when top link locomotives developed a fault which required a temporary removal from traffic, then engines from other regions were drafted in to cover the absence. Three such occasions come to mind: in 1951 the 'Britannia' Pacifics suffered driving wheels slipping on axles; in 1956 a number of the Western Region 'King' class 4-6-0 developed cracks in their front bogies. Third and between those dates was in 1953, when a Southern Region 'Merchant Navy' Pacific suffered a cracked driving axle, necessitating all the class being withdrawn for checks. Amongst replacements sent on loan to Nine Elms shed were six V2 class 2-6-2s from the Eastern Region: Nos.60893, 60908 and 60916 from New England, along with Nos.60896, 60917 and 60928 from Doncaster. They arrived at 70A on Thursday 14th May and were thrown straight in to work on the Region's prestige expresses. Within days of their arrival on the SR it was realised that clearance problems with the front steps might arise so all six had the steps removed whilst a temporary vertical bar was fitted on each side of the buffer beam to hold the cylinder drain pipes in place as they were previously attached to the steps. Here at Nine Elms shed is one of the Doncaster engines suitably altered on 26th June 1953, just two days before they returned to the ER. Note the V2 is still carrying the 36A shed plate; behind 'West Country' No.34019 BIDEFORD is perhaps standing guard over the stranger on its 'manor!' No.60917 was built at Darlington and put into traffic on 10th August 1940 as LNER No.4888, and No.917 from 16th December 1946. Allocated to Doncaster for most of its life, it also undertook a sixteen month residency at King's Cross during the early years of WW2 and then towards the end of the conflict it was reallocated to Gorton for two years. It was withdrawn from 36A on 13th April 1962, to be scrapped at the nearby works soon afterwards. *David Dalton.*

The latter days of steam numerously brought 'foreign' locomotives in valedictory services, to new places throughout Britain. One such was when the Locomotive Club of Great Britain's *A2 COMMEMORATIVE TOUR* of Sunday 14th August 1966, saw one of the last surviving Peppercorn A2 Pacifics No.60532 BLUE PETER come all the way from Aberdeen Ferryhill shed, to London Waterloo. It was intended to run via the LSWR main line to Exeter, then via Taunton, Westbury, Salisbury and Basingstoke, back to Waterloo. Your scribe saw the A2 at Clapham Junction on the outward journey and a fine sight and sound it was, but unfortunately, 60532 did not perform so well and had to come off the train at Westbury on the return, from where Britannia No.70004 WILLIAM

SHAKESPEARE took over, via Salisbury and Basingstoke, to London. In happier moments, the day before its breakdown, No.60532 poses in immaculate condition, in the yard of Nine Elms shed. Blue Peter the horse won four major races in his first year, 1939, including the 2000 Guineas and Derby, but his career was then cut short by World War 2. *P.J. Robinson (ARPT).*

THE END! **In this section we feature the last months leading up to the end of main line steam on the Southern Region, at Nine Elms engine shed, on 9th July 1967.** This was a poignant time for all lovers of the steam locomotive: the end of main line steam in London and the last steam on the Southern, which is somewhat ironic, considering the Southern Railway and afterwards, led the way to modernising its motive power with the aim of eradicating steam! The Bulleid Pacifics, Standard Class 5 4-6-0s and others, went out in a blaze of glory, when the mostly young crews then working steam, really pushed their steeds in feats of speed. More than a few 100mph+ runs were recorded and considering the final condition of the locomotives involved it was a massive tribute not only to their designers, their re-builders and lastly, to the men that kept them running in their end days. On the other side of the coin as it were, 'Joe Public' was then very pleased to see the end of 'those dirty, smelly, old-fashioned machines.' *Sic Transit Gloria* was the Latin expression used at the time – The Glory Has Passed. But all we will say is that when a steam locomotive is in action today, just observe how Joe Public comes out in droves to watch and ride. The magic, if anything, is now even stronger: *Non Transibit Gloria* – the glory has not passed!

February 1967 and although it has only two months of service left, un-rebuilt 'West Country' No.34002 SALISBURY (formerly), receives considerable attention at Nine Elms, with two sets of driving wheels out and no doubt much work being done, out of sight of the camera. Just look at what would then have been considered normal conditions for undertaking heavy, dirty and sometimes, dangerous labour – Health & Safety, grind your teeth and weep! The 4-6-2 had been a 70A engine since January 1965, having been built at Brighton in June 1945. *P.J. Robinson (ARPT).*

Even with the end of steam in sight, the interior of Nine Elms still presented a marvellous vista. Among the denizens of the 1910 building in May 1967 were sadly, two un-identified locomotives: a rebuilt Light Pacific and a BR Std. Cl.3 2-6-2T. However, the latter can only have been 82019 or 82029, because they were the only two of the type to remain at Nine Elms all through 1967, up to July; both were withdrawn on the last day. However, Ivatt Cl.2 No.41312 is identified. The locomotive had been delivered new from Crewe in May 1952, to Faversham depot. It remained in the Southern Region, coming to Nine Elms in April 1967, from Bournemouth. It too was withdrawn on the last day and is today preserved in working order, on the Mid-Hants Railway. *P.J. Robinson (ARPT).*

Thanks to the science of photography, a moment in time is captured – that piece of coal will forever remain suspended, between the fireman's hands and the front of the tender of 'Merchant Navy' No.35003 ROYAL MAIL. The date was June 1967 and who knows, might this it have been the very day that the locomotive forever entered the history books? No.35003 achieved the last authenticated (by a veritable trainload of performance recorders!), speed of over 100 m.p.h. by a British steam locomotive. On 26th June, with the end of steam just two weeks away, the Bulleid Pacific reached 105.88 m.p.h. while hauling a light train of three carriages and two vans, between Winchfield and Fleet. The fact that the vans were not passed for speeds above 90 m.p.h. did not seem to be of concern, but thus did steam say farewell! The 4-6-2 was built at Eastleigh in September 1941, rebuilt in August 1959 and withdrawn 9th July 1967; despite its achievement, the engine did not escape the cutter's torch. Royal Mail Line Ltd. was formed in 1932 and operated mostly in the Atlantic to South America, the West Indies and through the Panama Canal, north to Vancouver, Canada. It was taken over in 1965 by Furness, Withy & Co. and by 1972 the name Royal Mail had disappeared as a separate line. *P.J. Robinson (ARPT).*

The artist David Shepherd, famed as 'The man who loves giants,' found artistic inspiration in the widely diverse subjects of elephants and steam locomotives. In one of his periods of activity, he vividly and sadly captured the atmosphere of Nine Elms' battered and decaying buildings and the last remaining locomotives therein. In this valedictory picture we see the artist's easel and the two oil drums he used as a seat and a rest for some of his materials. The date is around March 1967 and three locomotives are identified, from left to right: BR Std. Cl.4 No.80012, which came to 70A from Eastleigh in October 1965 and was withdrawn in February 1967; rebuilt 'West Country' No.34047 CALLINGTON (formerly) built Brighton November 1946, rebuilt October 1958, withdrawn June 1967; finally, BR Std. Cl.4 No.76064 delivered new, from Doncaster in July 1956, to Eastleigh, where it spent all its working life to withdrawal on 9th July 1967. *D.R. Dunn coll. (ARPT).*

STEWARTS LANE

This, the first Capital shed of the London Chatham & Dover Railway (LCDR), opened in February 1862 and followed contemporary American practice in the provision of a large, open turntable roundhouse of no less than forty roads, of which twenty were covered, twenty were open to the elements; four of the open tracks allowed access to the turntable. At first the depot was known by the name of Longhedge, reflecting the LCDR's locomotive works of that name which stood nearby. In 1881 the roundhouse was swept away and in what must have been a difficult transition period, it was replaced on the same site by a sixteen road, dead-end brick building with a roof of five transverse pitches.

Thus it remained, until a massive SR development plan of the early-mid 1930s (when the name Stewarts Lane first came into use, instead of Longhedge or Battersea), saw the depot receive a mechanical coaling plant and a water softener, serving many more water columns than hitherto. Even more so, at the same time, the roof was reconstructed in a different style of northlight, with eight longitudinal pitches, each covering two roads – a unique application.

Stewarts Lane, 'The Lane' as it was commonly known, was several times damaged during WW2, but generally survived well. Under the SR it was coded BAT then under BR Southern Region, 73A and in its final steam days, incongruously as 75D. The coming of electric locomotives in 1959 presaged the end of steam, which with further electric and diesel power, came in September 1963. Stewarts Lane continued to serve the new order until 28th September 1997 when the diesel allocation moved away.

That was not the end though as in current times, with the old building reduced to just two roofed two road sections, plus lots of open sidings, it serves as a resting place for various diesel and electric locomotives and rolling stock and is the regular depot for the steam engines designated to haul prestige services like the present day, *ORIENT EXPRESS* and *BELMOND* Pullman trains. It still enjoys a depot code – SL. In presenting the following illustrations it should be commented that Stewarts Lane shed was challenging for the photographer. Panoramic pictures of the depot as a whole were difficult; it occupied a cramped site within a triangle of lines with above them, viaducts on the south, east and west side, and an enormous depository warehouse on the north. Everywhere, there were obstructive backgrounds, but for some of us, this just added to the intensity of the place!

This picture gives a reasonable idea of what Stewarts Lane shed looked like after its SR rebuilding. The date was Thursday 30th August 1956 and five of the eight longitudinal northlight pitches are seen, but looking at the gloomy interior of the building the light bit of 'northlight' was none too successful! Standing outside are two 73A locomotives, separated by a half-century. Class C No.31719 was built by Sharp Stewart & Co. in January 1901 and was a long-term resident, moving away only in May 1961 to Bricklayers Arms from where it would be withdrawn exactly one year later. Ivatt Cl.2 No.41292 came new to Stewarts Lane, from Crewe in November 1951 and would leave for the west in January 1961, going to Exmouth Junction. That depot would come into the Western Region in September 1963 and the 2-6-2T would be withdrawn in the same month. *Howard Foster.*

Stewarts Lane – What was on shed Sunday 15th June 1952:

8765, 30776, 31019, 31033, 31067, 31158, 31261, 31263, 31266, 31319, 31321, 31410, 31412, 31504, 31557, 31558, 31573, 31575, 31578, 31581, 31583, 31719, 31749, 31813, 31901, 31904, 31905, 31907, 31908, 31910, 31912, 31915, 32100, 32101, 32103, 32104, 32105, 32106, 32107, 32424, 33036, 34070, 34072, 34087, 34088, 34090, 34092, 34102, 34103, 35027, 35028, 41290, 41292, 41294, 41295, 41297, 42089, 42091, 42105, 70004, 70014

Total: 61.

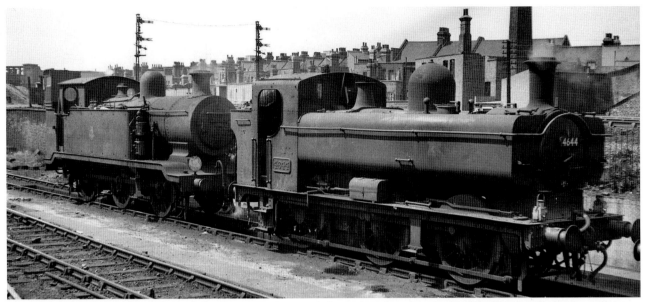

'The Lane' was another of those Southern sheds that frequently hosted engines from north of the Thames, having crossed over with inter-regional freights. Here is one such visitor in September 1952; GWR Pannier tank No.4644 from Old Oak Common; it would have travelled from Old Oak via the West London Joint line, crossing the Thames at Battersea railway bridge. It, and resident ex-LBSCR Class E2 No.32104, are parked on a dead-end siding near 73A's turntable, which was itself sited at the end of an out of the way spur – space was ever a premium at the shed! Note that No.4644 has faint remnants of GWR on its tanks, so almost certainly the engine had not undergone a major overhaul for at least four years. It was built at Swindon in January 1943, going new to Old Oak, which it left in February 1961, for Swindon. It soon went further west, ending up at far off Goodwick in November 1962 from where it was withdrawn eleven months later. Seven of the ten E2 tanks were based at Stewarts Lane at the time. Powerful for their size, one job that usually came their way was hauling the very heavy stock of *THE NIGHT FERRY* to and from Victoria. When it did this for a departure, the E2 acted as a banking engine to get the train up the sharp gradient to Grosvenor Bridge, over the Thames. No.32104 was built at Brighton in January 1914 and would be transferred to Southampton Docks shed in November 1961; it worked there until withdrawn in April 1963. *R.F. Payne (ARPT)*

During the fourth quarter of 1955, the last fifteen BR Std. Cl.4 4-6-0s, Nos.75065 – 75079, were delivered from Swindon works, to the Southern Region, five going to Dover and ten to Exmouth Junction. Seen at Stewarts Lane on Thursday 18th August 1960, wearing a Three Bridges shed plate is No.75070, one of the batch that first went to 72A (September 1955). It left there in June 1956 for Bath, Green Park, then Eastleigh and Brighton to find its way to 75E in January 1960. Further reallocations would bring it to Stewarts Lane before going on to Nine Elms and Eastleigh where it was condemned in September 1966, just eleven years old. The

bridge in the background, one of the three viaducts crossing the depot, carried the former SECR line out of Victoria, between Battersea Pier Junction and Wandsworth Road over the eastern end of the shed. Just getting into the picture is 'Schools' No.30923 BRADFIELD built in December 1933. One wonders if this engine was a bit of a pig because in BR times it would be reallocated no less than twelve times, between Bricklayers Arms, Dover, St. Leonards and Basingstoke, before it came to 73A in May 1959. Moved again in May 1961 to Bricklayers Arms and October the same year, to Brighton, No.30923 was withdrawn in December 1962. Bradfield School, now called Bradfield College, was founded in the Berkshire village of Bradfield, in 1850, initially for boys only, but today is co-educational for the 13-18 age group. The school motto is: *Benedictus es, O Dominie doce me Statuta Tua* (You are blessed, Lord: teach me your laws). *David J. Dippie.*

Stewarts Lane shed's main claim to fame was that it normally provided the locomotives for working the prestigious *GOLDEN ARROW* Pullman car express, between Victoria and Dover; only the depot's very best engines and crews were rostered for this duty. Such a locomotive, being made ready to haul the train on a dull and dingy Thursday 8th July 1954, was 'Battle of Britain' No.34071 601 SQUADRON. Built at Brighton in April 1948 the engine at first carried the name 615 SQUADRON but this was changed in August 1948 for unknown reasons, as *615 Squadron* would be allocated to sister engine No.34082, when it came out of the works at Brighton in September 1948 (*see* later picture). No.34071 went new to Dover shed and then transferred to Stewarts Lane in December 1949, only to return to Dover in June 1955. The Pacific left Dover in January 1961 for Nine Elms and then, in September 1964, moved on to Eastleigh. No.34071 was withdrawn in April 1967 as one of the un-rebuilt Bulleid Pacifics. 601 (County of London) Squadron was formed in 1925 and flew Hurricanes during the Battle of Britain, from Middle Wallop, Tangmere and Debden airfields; it was notable in that some of its pilots were the first Americans to fly for Great Britain during the war. *F.W. Hampson (ARPT).*

One could write an entire book about the *NIGHT FERRY* train, so what follows is necessarily brief. The service started on 5th October 1936 using *Compagnie Internationale des Wagon-Lits* rolling stock specially constructed for the train and adapted to fit the British loading gauge. Because of the complicated activity loading and unloading the train's carriages onto and off the cross-Channel ferry boats, timekeeping was generally erratic, but the traditional timetable was: Victoria – depart 2100; Dover Marine – arrive 2242; Dunkerque – depart 0534; Paris Nord – arrive 0900. Paris Nord – depart 2200; Dunkerque – arrive 0121; Dover Marine – depart 0720; Victoria – arrive 0910. The *NIGHT FERRY* was suspended during WW2 but recommenced on 5th December 1947. Because of the weight of the train in post-war years it was the only service on the Southern Region to regularly be double-headed, by a Bulleid Pacific and an E1 or L class 4-4-0. All of which brings us to this picture of Class L1 No.31754 on Sunday 8th May 1955, against the background of Messrs Hampton and Sons' huge depository. The 4-4-0 carries a *NIGHT FERRY* headboard so doubtless its home depot at Dover, had turned it out to pilot a Bulleid 4-6-2 on that morning's Up train. One can assume it would perform a similar duty that evening with the Down working, as always leaving Victoria's platform 2, where customs inspections were carried out before departure. Steam was replaced on the train at the end of the 1950s, until aged rolling stock and cheap air travel brought about the end of the iconic service on 31st October 1980. The Class L was built in 1926 by NBL (Works Number 23357) and would transfer from Dover to Nine Elms in May 1959, at which shed it was stored until withdrawal in November 1961. *F.W. Hampson (ARPT).*

As remarked earlier, stabling space at Stewarts Lane was always a problem. Here are Class E2 No.32101 and another locomotive, occupying the spur into the depot's wheel-drop, while behind, other engines are stabled in and around the weighbridge, the roof of which is just seen, all beneath the towering mechanical coaler. It was another gloomy day at 73A, Saturday 3rd May 1952 while the E2 sits in steam waiting for its next duty – perhaps handling the stock of the *GOLDEN ARROW* or *NIGHT FERRY*. The engine would be among the first three of the class (with Nos.32108 and 32109, both from Dover shed), to be moved to Southampton Docks. That would be in January 1957 from where the engine was taken out of service in September 1962. *F.W. Hampson (ARPT)*.

Stewarts Lane's 300-ton capacity coaler dominates the skyline, even putting Hampton's depository in the shade as it were. And shade there would have been on an unusually sunny day in August 1952, as Class U1 No.31901 is made ready to go off-shed for its next duty. The 3-cylinder Mogul had been built at Eastleigh in June 1931 and like all the class it spent almost all its working life in the Eastern and Central sections of the SR, when in WW2, the U1's dimensions allowed them to perform on the Hastings line where they were particularly turned out to work troop trains. As hinted

No.31901 did stray when, with sister 31902, they left their usual haunts in June 1961, upon transfer to Exmouth Junction. They remained there until December 1962 before transferring to Brighton, their performances in Devon and Cornwall not having shown any significant advantage over other types employed there; No.31901 was withdrawn from 75A in June 1963. Behind the U1 is 'Battle of Britain' No.34089 602 SQUADRON which was built in December 1948, going new, to Ramsgate and from there to Stewarts Lane in May 1951. Six months later came a most interesting diversion when, together with four other Bulleid Light Pacifics: Nos.34039 BOSCASTLE, 34057 BIGGIN HILL, 34065 HURRICANE and 34076 41 SQUADRON, No.34089 was transferred to 30A Stratford depot, to replace the Eastern Region BR Britannia Pacifics, temporarily withdrawn for correction of axle problems. All five Light Pacifics returned to the SR between March and June 1952. 602 (City of Glasgow) Squadron was formed in 1925, equipped with Spitfires in 1939 and fought in the Battle of Britain from RAF West Hampnett, in West Sussex. The squadron motto is: *Cave leonum cruciatum* (Beware the crossed lion). *K.H. Cockerill (ARPT)*.

Two more locomotives stabled out of the way on that spur near Stewarts Lane's turntable, on Sunday 18th September 1960. Local resident W 2-6-4T No.31914 sits outside a visitor from Hornsey shed in the shape of J50 No.68917. The bridge above the locomotives carried the former LBCSR line out of Victoria, between Battersea Park Junction and Factory Junction, over the western end of the shed. The 2-6-4T is seen in Volume One of this series, in the section dealing with 70B Feltham in 1964, where the locomotive was then resident. In this picture No.31914 was still a long-term member of 73A's roster, but it would leave in three months on transfer to Norwood Junction; then from there to Exmouth Junction in November 1962, returning to Norwood in September 1963; it would move from 75C to 70B in December 1963. Hornsey's J50 is an interesting locomotive: Built at Doncaster in August 1919 (works No.1499), it spent many years at Ardsley shed before transferring to Doncaster on 28th November 1948. The 0-6-0T moved to Hornsey on 19th October 1952 and worked from there until the diesels began arriving at 34B at which point the J50 went back to 36A in July 1961. At 36A it was taken out of Capital Stock on 16th September 1962, to join Eastern Region Departmental Stock as No.12. It was then employed as a shunting engine within the works at Doncaster, a duty performed until finally being condemned 30th May 1965. It was sold for scrap in July 1965. *N.W. Skinner (ARPT).*

As if the yard of Stewarts Lane shed was not cluttered enough, there was a post-war addition of a carriage cleaning shed, which is seen in this picture of 'King Arthur' No.30768 SIR BALIN standing outside. The date was Tuesday 21st May 1957, a day on which Mr Sanderson took many fine pictures around 73A, as will be seen below. No.30768 was another of the 'Scotch Arthurs' (NBL 23214/ June 1925), and had been a Stewarts Lane engine since transfer from Dover in June 1951. It would depart in May 1959 for Nine Elms, from where it would operate until withdrawal in October 1961. Sir Balin (full title: Sir Balin le Savage) was also known as the Knight with the Two Swords. He came from Northumberland and was an early presence and departure in the legend of Arthur. For some reason imprisoned by Arthur, Sir Balin is freed and meets a mysterious girl bearing a sword that only the most virtuous knight may draw. Sir Balin does this, but soon after he and his brother, Sir Balan (No.30769) kill each other in single combat, thereby fulfilling an earlier prophecy about the bearer of the damsel's sword. *C.J.B. Sanderson (ARPT).*

Stewarts Lane – What was on shed Saturday 15th February 1958:
30766, 30767, 30769, 30793, 30794, 30795, 30908, 30909, 30915, 31019, 31064, 31145, 31178, 31261, 31265, 31409, 31411, 31413, 31550, 31551, 31575, 31578, 31582, 31584, 31686, 31691, 31719, 31810, 31811, 31897, 31914, 31921, 32102, 32106, 32455, 34067, 34068, 34082, 34091, 34092, 34097, 34101, 35015, 41292, 42074, 42080, 42086, 42087, 42090, 42091, 73080, 73081, 73083, 73084, 73085, 73088, 80149   Total: 57.

The middle step of what was once considered (still is? – if it can be afforded?), the only path for someone who really wants to be 'someone' in British society: i.e. Eton – Harrow – Oxbridge! Wide chimney Schools No.30919 HARROW was visiting from Dover shed and is stabled beside Stewarts Lane's wheel-drop; the building just visible at left was the weigh shed. The 4-4-0 was built in June 1933, and is residing at 73A on Thursday 21st May 1957, and would transfer to Nine Elms in May 1959 and on from there, to Brighton, in April 1960; withdrawal would follow nine months later! Also seen is N class No.31812, built at Ashford in August 1920 and a long-term Stewarts Lane resident. It would be transferred in the big May 1959 shake-up of Southern Region steam, to Guildford and from there to Exmouth Junction in August 1963. Withdrawal, courtesy of the Western Region, occurred in July 1964. Founded in 1243 and granted a Royal Charter in 1572, Harrow school still today caters for boys only, as does its essential predecessor in the ladder of education, Eton. For such a pillar of the British way of life (in some peoples' eyes anyway), Harrow school has not one, but two mottoes: *Stet Fortuna Domus* (Let the Fortune of the House Stand) and *Donorum Dei Dispensatio Fidelis* (The Faithful Dispensation of the Gifts of God). *C.J.B. Sanderson (ARPT).*

Stewarts Lane's coaling and ash pilot on Thursday 21st May 1957 was Class H No.31261 which was built at Ashford in November 1905. The 0-4-4T was allocated to 73A for all its BR service, leaving only when withdrawn, in October 1961. In the middle background a trio of tenders may be seen: a Bulleid Light Pacific, Britannia No.70004 (*see* next illustration), and another BR Standard; there is also a good glimpse of 73A's unusually laid out roof. In the far background at left, a 4-SUB electric multiple unit is crossing the Battersea Pier Junction to Wandsworth Road viaduct. *C.J.B. Sanderson (ARPT).*

Stewarts Lane – What was on shed Sunday 25th February 1962:

4631, 31410, 31411, 31510, 31542, 31588, 31823, 31824, 31899, 34089, 34100, 75069, 76060, 80031, 80068, 80081, E5000, E5009, E5013, E5014, E5015, E5016, E5017, E5018, E5022, 20002, D2253, 11226(D2256), D2284, D2398, D3049, D3472, D6576, D6577   Total: 34.

No. 30768 has moved out of the way of the washing plant, to allow BR Standard Class 7 No.70004 WILLIAM SHAKESPEARE take centre stage, fully dressed and ready to haul the *GOLDEN ARROW* express on Thursday 21st May 1957. One of two 'Britannia' Pacifics allocated to Stewarts Lane in June and September 1951. Until they both left in June 1958, they were used whenever possible for the *GOLDEN ARROW*, but also appeared on other boat trains. The staff at 73A took special care of the engines, making sure they were kept in the best mechanical and decorative condition, and only the most senior crews were given the boat train duties. Even so the locomotive seems to be oozing a bit of steam from the regulator gland at the left rear of the smoke box although the super-shine finish to the paintwork is exemplary. No.70004 entered traffic from Crewe in April 1951, going first to the Eastern Region at Stratford, before transferring regions and moving to Stewarts Lane in September that year. Upon departure from 73A, the engine went to the London Midland Region at Trafford Park depot. It saw eight further transfers within the LM Region, ending at Kingmoor shed in June 1967; it was withdrawn from there at the end of that year. In the background see that Messrs. Hampton and Sons' warehouse is undergoing renovation. *C.J.B. Sanderson (ARPT).*

To finish what must have been a marvellous visit to Stewarts Lane on that Thursday in May 1957, Mr Sanderson walked across the tracks toward Hampton's depository to capture this interesting picture. The Pullman Observation Car seated twenty-seven passengers and was equipped with a bar for a drinks service. It was one of two that had been converted from earlier passenger vehicles in 1947, and numbered 13 and 14, for the introduction of the Southern Railway's prestigious all-Pullman *DEVON BELLE* train. That ran from Waterloo to Exeter, where it divided into two portions, for Plymouth and Ilfracombe. The service commenced on 20th June 1947 and BR Southern Region continued the workings until poor passenger numbers caused the Plymouth portion to be dropped in September 1949. The train carried on running to Ilfracombe, but really it was not a success so it too ceased in September 1954, at the end of the summer timetable. The observation cars had always been used on the Ilfracombe section of the *DEVON BELLE* and after that train ceased, they transferred to the LM Reg. where they were included in such formations as *THE WELSH CHIEFTAIN* land cruise, and other charter trains. In 1961 they were moved to Scotland for use on the Inverness-Kyle of Lochalsh and Glasgow-Oban lines. When that all ended the cars were returned to England where today both still exist, in use by two preserved railways: Car No.13 is with the Dartmouth Steam Railway and No.14 runs on the Swanage Railway. It is not known which of the two cars is depicted here, but it is apparent that the guard's van partly seen at right was built for the LNER, had a plated number of 268956 and last received mechanical attention in April 1957! *C.J.B. Sanderson (ARPT).*

In Volume One of this series, in the section on Feltham, is a picture of T9 No.30719 of Nine Elms shed with the comments that the locomotive typically was used for trip and inter-yard workings. That was in April 1952 and here on Saturday 3rd May 1958, a year before it would leave 70A for Exmouth Junction, No.30719 is still employed on trip duties (note that since the visit to Feltham the T9 had been to works and now had the BR emblem and power classification painted on). This time it is propelling wagons into the top end of the shed yard; note that the LMR 12-ton box van has Nine Elms chalked on the door. To help the reader orientate, there were two 'official' entrances to Stewarts Lane shed: on the west side, from Silverthorne Road, through the former Longhedge Works; on the east side, from Corunna Terrace, over a footbridge into the top of the depot yard (invariably having to avoid dozens of trainspotters!). This picture is taken from that footbridge just before it passes under the ex-SECR viaduct; the junction at right, with the shadow of the signal box, is Stewarts Lane Junction and ahead is the bridge carrying the LSWR main lines to Waterloo. *W.R.E. Lewis (ARPT).*

In an earlier caption it was told how BB No.34071 carried the name 615 SQUADRON for a short time before being renamed, and how the relinquished name was, a few months later, allocated to another 'BB'. Well, here it is: No.34082 615 SQUADRON in rebuilt form, in the coaling and ash cleaning area at Stewarts Lane on Monday 27th June 1960, where one of the shed staff undertakes the job of shovelling the discarded ash into wagons; not all things Age of Steam could be called romantic! The raised tracks in the background were the ex-LBSCR and SECR lines from Stewarts Lane Junction, to Longhedge B and C Junctions, where they met end-on, with the West London Extension Joint Railway. Then, just visible at left, through the former LBSCR bridge arch is that spur mentioned in previous captions where visitors from 'Norf' London were usually stabled. No.615 (County of Surrey) Squadron formed in 1937 and during the Battle of Britain flew Hurricanes in two stints, from Kenley and Northolt, with a rest period in between at Prestwick, Scotland. The squadron's nickname was 'Churchill's Own' and its motto: *Conjunctis viribus* (By our united force). *Howard Foster.*

In a previous caption about Britannia No.70004, it was told that two of the BR Class 7s were stationed at Stewarts Lane – here is the other one, on Sunday 20th October 1957. Just like her sister, No.70014 IRON DUKE is in absolutely first-rate condition, ready to haul the *GOLDEN ARROW*. As also told earlier, both 'Brits' left 73A in September 1958, initially to Trafford Park. No.70014 then undertook no fewer than *twelve* reallocations around the LM Region before finishing at Kingmoor, in August 1966. For the British Iron Duke means Sir Arthur Wellesley, first Duke of Wellington, leader of the allied army that defeated Napoleon at Waterloo in 1815 and later a Prime Minister. *David J. Dippie coll.*

Having just mentioned the two 'Brit's' and their working of the *GOLDEN ARROW*, here is a day when neither of them were available – Friday 5th August 1955 – rostered instead for the train was WC No.34103 CALSTOCK, which had been based at Stewarts Lane since arriving new in February 1950. The Pacific would remain a 73A locomotive until November 1956, when it transferred to Dover, leaving that place in January 1961 for Bournemouth, and moving on to Eastleigh in September 1964; exactly two years later No.34103 was withdrawn. Also seen in the picture is BB No.34074 46 SQUADRON built at Brighton in May 1948, which after a few early moves of depot, ended up at Dover in February 1951. Thus, it was a 74C engine when this picture was taken. *Norman Preedy.*

NORWOOD JUNCTION

The Southern Railway carried on the progressive ideas of its antecedents with a programme of electrification, applied as quickly as funds allowed. The remaining steam locomotives were not forgotten, however, and following the examples set at Feltham and Hither Green, the marshalling yards at Norwood Junction were modernised to cater for primarily cross-London traffic. A single road engine shed had existed in LBSCR days, opened at a date unknown and closed in 1907; it was sited south of the station on the Down side. However, the revamped marshalling yard required the provision of an engine shed and this was accomplished in 1935 with the opening of a five road dead-end shed in concrete and asbestos, under a northlight roof. Norwood Junction shed was situated north of the station on the Down side, in a somewhat cramped location between the main line and a spur connecting West Norwood and Norwood Junction. The depot was equipped with a water softener, 65 foot turntable at the rear and a single-sided, ramped coaling stage that flanked the main line.

The depot was known for its fleet of shunting engines of ex-LBSCR 0-6-2T classes E4 and E6, but also for housing the only four E4X and the only two E6X. Even so, the ever modern-minded SR introduced its first diesel shunting locomotives in 1937, designed by Maunsell specifically for working in Norwood Junction's yards. Initially termed as experimental, the diesels were deemed to be a success overall and after the war were joined by more machines to the design of Bulleid. Thus was Norwood Junction given an early warning of its own demise when, following BR's rapid adoption of diesel traction from the late 1950s, the depot was closed on 5th January 1964, after less than twenty-nine years operation.

The depot was coded NOR by the Southern Railway and then 75C by British Railways, the shed buildings were removed in 1966 and today a railway engineering maintenance depot occupies the site.

Taken from the footbridge that was the only access to Norwood Junction shed, via a cinder path leading from Penge Road, is this panorama from Sunday 6th September 1959. The shed was quite full but only three types of steam locomotive can readily be identified: Class W 2-6-4T, Class C2X 0-6-0 and at least one Class K 2-6-0; also one of Bulleid's 0-6-0DE shunting engines. In the far left distance, Bromley Junction signal box can be seen; among other things it controlled the spur coming round the right hand edge of the depot, to Norwood Junction. The nearest building in the shed yard was an early 1950s construction, providing doubtless much appreciated canteen and office space, where previously a grounded coach body had been employed. Also seen, a small group of enthusiasts is about to start writing down engine numbers! *T.J. Edgington.*

Norwood Junction – What was on shed Sunday 18th May 1952:
30533, 30534, 30539, 30546, 30547, 31916, 31917, 31919, 31920, 32340, 32344, 32407, 32411, 32414, 32416, 32417, 32443, 32444, 32466, 32476, 32477, 32478, 32489, 32544, 32545, 32547, 15201, 15213, 15216, 15218, 15235   Total: 31.

One of only four, Class E4X 0-6-2T No.32466 sits on the coaling road at Norwood Junction on Sunday 22nd October 1950. The unidentified locomotive behind the 0-6-2T, with SOUTHERN just visible through the grime on its tanks, was a Class E4 and it is easy to see the difference in height of the two locomotives' boilers – that of the E4X is much higher pitched and is necessarily fitted with a shorter, Billinton chimney. No.32466 was built at Brighton as an E4, in April 1898, carrying for its first few years, the name HONOR OAK; it was rebuilt to E4X in February 1909. A long-term resident of Norwood Junction depot, along with sisters Nos.32477, 32478, and 32489, our subject would leave 75C after being withdrawn in December 1958. *K.H. Cockerill (ARPT)*

A few minutes after taking his picture of No.32466, Mr Cockerill walked up to the shed yard and found this: Class W No.31920 has BRITISH RAILWAYS on its tanks and BR number in Southern style figures, while behind, sister No.31916 has its BR number also in SR form, but retains SOUTHERN; the period of transition from privately-owned to publicly-owned was obviously lengthy! Behind the six-coupled tanks is that grounded coach body mentioned above – by its appearance it must have been quite insalubrious and well past its replacement date, hence its imminent demise! Both engines were built at Ashford in 1935; No.31916 in April, No.31920 in August. They were stationed at Norwood Junction at the time with No.31920 remaining so until withdrawn in July 1963. No.31916 would leave 75C in February 1953, for Hither Green, moving from there in May 1961 to Eastleigh and from there to Exmouth Junction in November 1962; it was also taken out of service in July 1963. *K.H. Cockerill (ARPT)*

One of Norwood Junction's Class E6 0-6-2Ts No.32416 basks in the sun on Saturday 7th June 1958; it is joined by Class Q No.30545. Twelve E6 class were built at Brighton between December 1904 and December 1905; the first eight carried names initially and it was two of those that were rebuilt to E6X in 1911: LBSCR Nos.407 and 411, WORPLESDON and BLACKHEATH, respectively. The engine depicted here came out of Brighton in November 1905. It commenced its BR career at Norwood Junction then it put in three years at Eastleigh, September 1950 – September 1953, before returning to 75C. In June 1959 No.32416 moved to Bricklayers Arms and from there to Feltham in January 1961; withdrawal came in February of the following year. The Class Q looks to be ex-works but is much defaced by that terrible stovepipe chimney! Note that it bears a NOT TO BE MOVED sign, so had something got a bit out of adjustment, post shopping? At the time the picture was taken No.30545 was based at Horsham, from where it would be transferred to Three Bridges in July 1959. Its last move came in January 1961, to Nine Elms, where it was withdrawn in May 1965. *C.J.B. Sanderson (ARPT)*.

Class C2X No.32544 is 'top and tailed' by a Drewry diesel-mechanical shunter and a Q class 0-6-0, while a W class 2-6-4T stands at the side. This was a typical mix of motive power that could be seen at 75C from the end of the 1950s – the date was actually July 1960. Built as a Class C2 in December 1901, LBSCR No.544 would be rebuilt to a C2X in January 1911 and by the dawn of BR found itself at Horsham shed. The locomotive left there in April 1951 for Norwood Junction, where it spent the rest of its days, to withdrawal in November 1961. Looking up to the depot's 17000 gallon water tank, the water level indicator can be seen: the white painted plank with a cable connected to a float in the tank and ended with a black marker. The indicator worked in reverse – the lower the black marker against the white background, the higher the water in the tank. In other words, in this picture, the tank was nearly full, as was to be expected. *F.W. Hampson (ARPT)*.

Guy Fawkes Day 1959 (a Thursday) was already gloomy and smoky before millions of fireworks would add their by-products to the pollution! Class W No.31919 had just arrived on-shed and was making its way to the coal stage to be refuelled ready for its next job. A good view is again had of the depot's water tank (full!) and in the distance, the water softening plant. It may be seen from some of the illustrations here that there usually was a line of mixed wagons on the siding leading to the turntable – as seen behind the 2-6-4T. They served mixed purposes: receptacles for discarded ash, chemicals into, and sludge out of, the softening plant and the box wagons were used for ENPARTS – engine parts, to enable local repairs to be made. The 3-cylinder Class W was built at Ashford in June 1935 and would be a Norwood Junction engine for all its BR days; that ended with it being condemned in November 1963 – on Bonfire Night perhaps....? *Norman Preedy.*

Late afternoon sunshine on Monday 17th September 1962, nicely lights Class N No.31814 and a somewhat grubby, unidentified sister. The 2-6-0 was visiting Norwood Junction from Salisbury, making it a fairly rare appearance at 75C by a locomotive from that shed. Probably the Mogul had been borrowed by another depot for the turn to Norwood and doubtless it would find its way back to 72B on its next working – or two. The engine had been built at Ashford in November 1920 and would remain based at Salisbury until August 1963 when it would be transferred to the part-roundhouse shed at Guildford, from where it was condemned in July 1964. *Norman Preedy.*

Norwood Junction – What was on shed Sunday 25th February 1962:

31820, 31826, 31890, 31896, 31898, 31900, 31902, 31903, 31904, 31905, 31906, 31908, 31909, 31910, 31914, 31917, 31918, 31919, 31920, 31921, 31925, 80150, 15203, 15211, D2278, D2279, D2280, D2294, D3046, D3223, D3224, D3460, D3461, D3465, D4102, D4104

Total: 36.